High Performance Agencies

The Entrepreneurial Model for Parks, Recreation, and Tourism Organizations

Paul A. Gilbert

SAGAMORE
P U B L I S H I N G

Publishers: Joseph J. Bannon and Peter L. Bannon
Director of Sales and Marketing: William A. Anderson
Marketing Coordinator: Misty Gilles
Journals Marketing Manager: Emily Wakefield
Director of Development and Production: Susan M. Davis
Technology Manager: Keith Hardyman
Production Coordinator: Amy S. Dagit
Graphic Designer: Julie Schechter

ISBN print edition: 978-1-57167-770-9
ISBN ebook: 978-1-57167- 771-6
LCCN: 2014941114

Sagamore Publishing
1807 N. Federal Dr.
Urbana, IL 61801
www.sagamorepub.com

To Laura, Jenna, and Kiera, for their support of me in writing this book.

And to all of the amazing people I have had the honor to work with in this field who have inspired this work.

Contents

Section IV

Section V

Foreword

by Barbara Tulipane
President and CEO
National Recreation and Park Association

I met Paul Gilbert early in my tenure as the president of the National Recreation and Park Association (NRPA), and his thoughts regarding what makes a successful, high performing public park agency resonate with me. In fact, his ideas about leadership, operations, and service mirrored those of many highly successful executives in the high tech industry that I had just left to come to NRPA. So when Paul asked me to write the foreword for a new book he was writing on an entrepreneurial model for park and recreation agencies, I eagerly accepted his invitation.

Paul is a remarkable individual. Not only is he the executive director of a 12,000-acre multi-jurisdiction park agency in the booming Northern Virginia suburbs of metropolitan Washington, D.C., but he is also the author of many articles, blog posts, op-eds, and commentaries on a wide range of subjects. He has written a highly regarded book on leadership lessons from the Civil War entitled *Lead Like a General*. Paul is an energetic and visionary leader in the field of parks and recreation, and he has a vast curiosity about what makes parks, recreation, and tourism agencies successful and what causes them to sometimes fail.

During my early conversations with Paul, I didn't understand the complexities of the field of park and recreation well, and I found Paul's insightful analysis to be very helpful. What I came to realize was that unlike executives in the business community, park and recreation leaders have the challenge and responsibility of not only running a highly diversified organization, but they have the additional responsibility of meeting the needs of their constituents while protecting a community's natural resources, often in the context of an ever-changing political environment.

My dialogue with Paul has continued over the years, and I am continually uplifted by his original thinking and fresh approach to problem solving. He tackles complex problems and difficult issues such as leadership, performance, and reinvention with gusto, and he dissects thorny problems with the skill of a surgeon. Paul steadfastly maintains that the best path to success when meeting challenges is staying positive, not fixating on problems, and continually looking for solutions as conditions change.

The publication of this book is very timely for the park, recreation, and tourism industry. Paul provides clarity and a vision for the future based on lessons learned from the unprecedented budget cuts that agencies have experienced as a result of the financial crisis and the subsequent Great Recession. He explores why some agencies fared better than others through the economic downturn, and more importantly, why some agencies actually thrived during this difficult time. He poses a fundamental question: What made the agencies that succeeded different? Was it luck, a special dedicated revenue source, a voter-approved tax, a donor with deep pockets, or as Paul suggests, good leaders delivering high performance within a great supporting structure?

Public parks and recreation face extraordinary challenges today. Tax-supported general fund revenues for this public good are declining at a precipitous rate, and the trend shows no sign of abating. In fact, it is likely to grow. Greater demands are being placed on park and recreation leaders to develop sustainable new revenue sources while at the same time, public expectations are growing for more services and better programming.

Despite the trends, new opportunities beckon as well. There are excellent models emerging from high performance agencies on how parks, recreation, and tourism can contribute substantially to urban economic development and revitalization; strategies of how parks and recreation can be integral to planning and implementing individual and community health outcomes; and how parks can play a central role in creating livable, sustainable communities. These may be challenging times for parks and recreation, but they are also exciting times, and this book explores in detail what it takes to create and sustain a high-performance agency using an entrepreneurial model as a means to doing so.

I agree with Paul that the future for park and recreation professionals is bright, but only for those who embrace an entrepreneurial approach. Paul identifies in explicit terms how you need to get from where you are now to where you want to be. He identifies a clear path on how to create an indispensably important organization, one that creates healthy, attractive, and economically important public spaces that enrich the life of communities and attract businesses and residents alike. He tells how you can look to develop new sources of revenue and how you can position your agency to be customer-centric, constantly improving, and successfully meeting the future through innovation and reinvention.

You can use this book to learn how to build a creative, mission-focused team and identify methods to establish a culture where risk is not just tolerated, but accepted and celebrated. Perhaps most importantly, you can use this book to learn how to create an agency that is nimble enough to meet unknown yet inevitable challenges, but which is also sustainable and stable enough to ensure long-term success and high performance by embracing entrepreneurial models.

Every community deserves the conservation of its natural resources, daily access to healthy spaces and places, and the commitment of a society that provides equitable access for all. Public parks and recreation provide all these opportunities and have the ability to change lives and build better communities. This book is a manual on how to meet the challenges all park and recreation agencies face, and it is a manual for those in decision-making capacities to provide the leadership and vision that make our communities better. Such great potential can only be achieved through consistent high performance from the individuals and agencies that provide the public good that is parks and recreation. Thank you, Paul, for providing such a clear, concise road map on how all can get there.

Section I

Introduction

What is the Entrepreneurial Approach?

Merriam-Webster defines *entrepreneur* as **one who organizes, manages, and assumes the risks of a business or enterprise**.

The "risk" part of this definition implies a sense of ownership and investment that is far more than just someone who works for an organization. So if you have a sense of ownership and investment in the success of your organization, you are half way to being an entrepreneur. The other half is the "organize" and "manage" portions of the definition. This part implies active engagement in shaping the future. So if you have a sense of investment in the outcomes of your agency, and are willing to play a proactive role in shaping the future, you are an organizational entrepreneur!

Being willing to take risk, manage, and organize for the success of the organization means that you are willing to learn best practices from other fields that can help your agency. It means you are willing to engage in visioning and planning for future successes, as well as implementing the best methods of every element of your operations. Being an organizational entrepreneur has very little to do with where you are on the organizational chart and a great deal to do with attitude and willingness to create a brighter future.

Elements that will help in creating this brighter future include the following:

- constant reinvention;
- adopting the best management/leadership approaches, many of which are drawn from other fields;
- creating compelling missions and strategies that will drive the organization to new heights;
- creating a sustainable funding model;
- repositioning your agency to offer a new and more powerful value proposition to the public; and
- creating a performance-driven organization that motivates employees and adds value to the community.

What Does this Have to Do With Money?

On one level not much, and on another level, a great deal. You can be a passionate organizational entrepreneur even if your agency does not generate any enterprise revenue. Enterprise revenue (from business operation) is just one source of funding. If you represent a public agency that is serving the citizens and making the world a better place and you are invested in that outcome and pro-actively working for better results, then you are an entrepreneur. On the other hand, you can be with a highly profit-focused private enterprise, and if you do not have a sense of ownership and a willingness and desire to push for greater performance, you are not an entrepreneur.

The way this does relate to money is that whether your funding source is tax dollars or enterprise operations, for any organization to grow, develop, and serve its constituents/customers better, it needs to be funded. And generally when people in an organization are invested in the health of the agency, they start looking for ways to expand that vital funding. That might take the form of a lobbying campaign to increase the tax-funded budget of the agency, looking for increased grants and charitable contributions, or expanding enterprise operations.

If you have a sense of investment in the outcomes of your agency and are willing to play a proactive role in shaping the future

you are an organizational entrepreneur!

The chapters in this book on pricing and marketing are focused on enterprise operations, but all of the other chapters are applicable for organizations that aspire to improve regardless of their current funding mix. While the entrepreneurial approach focuses on organizational performance and is not explicitly about making money, I believe embracing this approach can lead to greater revenue generation in addition to higher staff morale, greater perceived community value, and a greater sense of progress.

While many of the examples are public-sector focused, all the fundamentals work the same whether the organization is a private sector company or a nonprofit organization. The concepts that help organizations thrive are universal.

A Time of Change

If you are in the parks, recreation, or tourism field, or any related field in the public, private, or nonprofit segments of our economy, you are aware that the field is undergoing a great deal of change. Some of these changes are due to economics, and some are due to a changing society. The age and ethnic makeup of society is changing, technology and fashion are changing the way people want to spend their time, and all of these factors mean that parks, recreation, and tourism agencies in the public, nonprofit, or for-profit segments need to change the way they do business to stay relevant and healthy.

Throughout the nation, many public agencies saw their taxpayer-supported budgets reduced during the recession of 2007–2011 and the slow recovery that followed. During this time, parks closed, and hours and staffing were reduced for many. A few stark examples of this include the following:

- Washington State set a multiyear plan to take its state park system from 60% funded out of the general fund (tax dollars) in 2007, to zero funding from the general fund by 2015. This would make it a 100% self-supported operation from user fees and enterprise operations.
- The city of Indianapolis considered privatizing its park and recreation department in 2014.

- The state of Ohio is considering using funds from oil and gas drilling in state parks to reduce the growing cost of unfunded maintenance needs in the park system.
- California closed 25% of its state parks in 2011 to address budget issues.

These are just a few examples of a larger shift. But it is not all gloom and doom; where there is change, there is always opportunity. Agencies adopting a nimble entrepreneurial approach are finding new ways of serving the public, while slow-moving bureaucratic organizations are in decline. This book seeks to lay out the essential elements for any agency (organization) to become better able to find the opportunities that exist in a changing environment and to create new growth and development.

Even if funding is not the primary challenge, every organization can improve its performance. By learning from the best in other fields' management and leadership, public agencies can improve their service delivery and value to the community. Strong and vibrant park and recreation agencies make for strong and vibrant communities. This book outlines many of the skills and approaches needed to improve the performance of any agency. If these entrepreneurial best practices are implemented, they can create strong and growing agencies that will build better communities. The world will be changed for the better, and people's lives will be improved if park and recreation agencies are seen as the powerful source of good that they can be. This book lays out a system of management and leadership that will lead us to this brighter future.

Organizational Life Cycle

When technology and other modes of operations are changing faster in the outside world than they are in your organization, you are living on borrowed time.

Organizations are like living organisms.

They are either growing or dying.

Mason Haire is credited with using the biological model of a living thing to describe the life stages of an organization (Haire & Posey, 1961). The theory of organizational life cycle (Figure 1) is that every organization is like a living being, experiencing birth, growth, maturity, and eventual decline and death. Whether looking at a new business start-up with a 2-year life or the Roman Empire with a 400-year life, every organization goes through the same phases.

As organizations enter the declining phase, they become more hierarchical in structure and more rule-bound and bureaucratic in operations. As this happens, they become less able to respond to external changes and become less valued and relevant to the world around them. At first glance, this may all seem very fatalistic, but it does not have to be. Some organizations spot the signs, break from the comfortable norm, and remake themselves with new products, services, and ways of doing things. This launches a new cycle. Those that do not seek proactive renewal will eventually fail. "The best way to predict the future is to create it," is a wonderful quote attributed to both Abraham Lincoln, as well as management guru Peter Drucker. Creating the future takes intentionality and a plan, and without those elements, business cycles and organizational dynamics can bring a rudderless organization down.

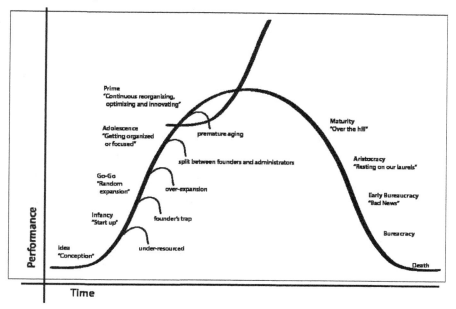

Figure 1. Organizational Life Cycle

Many might think that government entities last forever, but that is not the case. Agencies change over time, some are eliminated altogether, some see their mission change over time, and some are reorganized in new ways. All organizations must stay relevant and offer a high perceived value in the community in order to continue. It is important for every agency to self-examine where it is on the organizational life cycle regularly or risk slipping into decline.

Some large well-known private companies that no longer exist include the following:

- Compaq Computers
- PaineWebber Financial Advisors
- MCI WorldCom
- Standard Oil
- Arthur Andersen Accounting

There are many airlines and other companies that could be added to this list. Every one of these companies was a powerhouse in the economy with thousands of employees and a strong presence for decades. But each of them declined and eventually went out of business. Mergers, scandals, or just lack of profitability (bankruptcy) ended these once well-known companies.

Many parks and recreation agencies, whether local, state, or federal, public or nonprofit, have a long history of being in existence to serve a perceived set of "community needs," funded largely by tax dollars. The more static the perceived needs, the methods of service delivery, and the funding sources, the more likely the organization is to be in the declining phase of the organizational life cycle. Agencies need the freedom to not only start new programs and continue operations, but they must be able to face the more difficult task of eliminating programs, services, and ways of doing things that do not serve the public or respond to the market as well as they used to.

Charles Darwin is often attributed with having said, "It is not the strongest of the species who survives, nor the most intelligent, but the most responsive to change."

Figure 2. Evolution

Change Factors

Political Support

In North America, we have a number of very distinct cultural and political movements. Historically, many of these cultural/political divides could be plotted geographically on the map with red states and blue states. While there are still geographic differences, the increasing mobility of the population means that most areas will have some mix of political viewpoints.

The field of parks and recreation grew out of the idea of the "commons." In medieval England, the commons were areas of land that were communally owned and could be used by anyone. While most of us are not grazing our sheep or goats on the common land anymore, we are picnicking, hiking, and otherwise recreating on the common land we know as parks.

When the first English settlers arrived on Plymouth Rock, they had this notion of the commons. They came to America with the goal of setting up a better society. One of the first things these early settlers did when they started a new town was set up a taxing system and hire a school teacher. So the idea of taxpayer support for public services that would help to make a better society is among the early founding ideas of our nation. However, at the same time, other individuals and groups were coming to America not to create a better society, but to gain personal wealth in the wilderness. From this group came the equally rooted, self-focused libertarian philosophy of America.

One of these American values leads one to taxpayer-supported service for the common good, and the other to a low tax, and minimal service government model. These two ideologies have been competing for centuries and will continue for the foreseeable future. For parks, recreation, and tourism, the greatest challenge is when the tide changes and there is less political will to provide taxpayer-supported services to the public, a new funding model must be adopted. And when there is a desire to create a better society with taxpayer support, how are innovative programs developed that address the changing social needs? Both political movements require a nimble and innovative approach to service delivery to be successful.

Political will to support parks and recreation is also dramatically influenced by the value proposition that is being offered. If the essential argument for funding is that these are the same programs that have been historically supported, or worse, that these programs and services are for "leisure" (a term with little or no value associated with it), then the value proposition is low. If the programs and services are connected to high value items such as attracting tourism or new employers to the community, or a high return on investment on community health costs or other environmental costs that would be higher without parks and recreation, then you are offering a high value proposition.

Demographics

Every area is different, but in general, America is more ethnically diverse than it was 20 years ago, and the average age is higher than it used to be as the juggernaut baby boom generation moves toward traditional retirement age. In addition to the changing nature of the population, there is also the changing nature of how people want to spend their discretionary hours. Sports and other recreational activities, just as fashion, change over time. Additionally, and perhaps more importantly, how people spend their free time has changed with much more competition from technology than there used to be. The parks and recreation field is in a pitched competition for the public's time and money. Our success in attracting that time and money will have a lot to do with long-term success.

Technology

Information technology has transformed our lives in the last 20 years. Creative application of this new technology will be another area that separates those agencies that succeed from those that do not in the coming years.

Technology can transform the way park and recreation agencies interact with the public and market services. The same technology has the potential to transform how interpretation and educational messages are delivered. How and where people work and play is being transformed by a world where the lines between work and play are increasingly blurred. This will affect both the interaction with the public/customers as well as the role of supervising an increasingly "plugged-in" workforce.

The answers to all of the issues above rest in a new entrepreneurial approach to the management of parks, recreation, and tourism organizations.

The greatest challenge that the public field of parks and recreation faces is not so much the economy, politics, demographic or any other external challenge. The greatest challenge comes from risk-averse bureaucratic thinking. Organizations become ineffective when those in positions of influence stop being result-focused and start becoming process focused. Few games have ever been won by playing defense. It is only from a willingness to try new things and look at existing operations through new eyes that progress will come. For some, the positive, results-focused approach will come naturally, and for others it will challenge their thinking in a good way.

This book will highlight best management practices and show how to rejuvenate the field of parks, recreation, and tourism.

You Must Look to See

An Example of Selective Perception

THE POWER OF PERCEPTION

Focusing on opportunities or focusing on obstacles is more important than most people recognize. Two people can look at the same set of circumstances, and those who are pessimistically looking for all of the road blocks and obstacles will only see those things they are looking for. Another person who is looking for and expecting to see opportunities will most likely find them.

YouTube has a great video that demonstrates the power of perception. It is called the "Selective Attention Test" and is created by Daniel Simon and Christopher Chabris.

http://www.youtube.com/watch?v=vJG698U2Mvo

Being a Viking Agency

What is Your Approach to an Unsettled and Changing Environment?

From September 2010 to February 2012, there were a series of articles in NRPA's *Park & Recreation Magazine* using the analogy of Vikings vs. farmers. These articles were essentially a dialogue or debate about the future of the parks and recreation field in the modern era.

The metaphor is that of Vikings vs. farmers, with farmers focusing only on their fields, being excellent managers of their set resources, but not looking beyond the task of making the best of what resources they are given. The Vikings by contrast are more risk taking, exploring, opportunity seeking, and adaptable to a changing environment.

The basic premise is that the parks and recreation field has been managed in a stable governmental model for decades, but that the relatively stable environment of the past has shifted, and we have entered a more dynamic and ever-changing period. As a result of this shift, our approach to management needs to also shift if the field of parks and recreation is going to thrive. For this new era, we need a new, opportunity-seeking perspective. The passive manager, not focused beyond his facility or agency, will no longer be the model of success. This model of management is great when external forces are stable, but not great when the landscape is changing significantly. The role of these managers is very much like that of the farmer who is focused on the efficient management of his fields, but is not looking beyond what he knows.

In times of great change, a different set of skills and attitudes is needed for success, and those are the attributes of the Viking. Vikings were explorers and risk takers; they were looking to the horizon and seeking new opportunities. In the field of parks and recreation, the Vikings would be those leaders who are repositioning agencies, implementing new ways of doing things, embracing technological and demographic changes, and making parks and recreation facilities places of the future and not just the places of the past.

Part of being a Viking leader in parks and recreation is looking outside the parks and recreation field for new ideas and best practices. This book is an attempt to provide the skills and perspectives needed to be Viking leaders in parks and recreation.

In the field of management, we can learn a great deal from the best thinkers coming out of the top business/management schools in the world. To be efficient, effective, and serve the public in the best way, we need to constantly implement the best practices in management.

The change from the competent farmer tending his or her fields, or competent manager running the regular programs, to the Viking or industry leader looking for where and how the agency can be world class and innovative, is a major shift. Many people have trouble with change, but it is unlikely that the parks and recreation field will return to where it was in previous decades. So, change is about how to survive and thrive in the new world.

Look at the four pieces on Vikings and farmers and identify the different themes. The Viking/farmer theme will be referred to in later chapters of the book.

Are You a Viking or a Farmer?
Paul Gilbert

From *Parks & Recreation Magazine*, September 2010, p. 22

Legendary Norsemen didn't conquer the known world by doing things the way they had always been done. Nor should parks and recreation administrators.

The park and recreation field is undergoing great change. With state and local government budgets in great distress, a business as usual attitude is not a strategy for success. With many economists predicting that an end to the current recession will not come until sometime in 2013, what will parks and recreation look like at that point? Almost certainly, the agencies that survive and thrive will be those that chart new areas. These will be agencies with lean overhead and an entrepreneurial spirit. Agencies that show their value to the community in new and exciting ways and are less dependent on traditional sources of tax revenues will succeed. They will be Viking agencies.

From the late 8th into the 12th century, Vikings from Scandinavia were a dominant force in the world in and around Europe. They conquered vast areas and promoted trade. In the east, they set up the nation of Russia, and in the west they were the first Europeans to explore North America. Then, over time, they stopped exploring to become farmers, and the age of Vikings came to an end.

Most larger park agencies went through a Viking era, a period of time when leaders with foresight and a can-do attitude created opportunities which resulted in rapidly expanding lands and operations. Over time, any organization can become so focused on managing what they have that they forget to grow.

Management is much like farming. You have a set of operations, and you tend to those like a farmer tending his fields. There is a great tendency to do the same thing every year. It seems to work, and it becomes "how we always do things." There is nothing wrong with being a competent manager or farmer, so long as external forces do not change too rapidly. But when the way things have been done no longer addresses the changing circumstances, it is time to take to the "long boats" again.

While the farmer is focused on the management of a certain set of fields, the Viking is looking to the horizon for new opportunities. Successful Vikings were willing to take strategic risks and stretch themselves and their group to find the new opportunities. While they were seeking these new opportunities, they were not alone. Leif Ericson did not row to Newfoundland by himself; rather, he had a team of Vikings willing to try new things and take risks together for a shared reward.

"Going Viking," therefore, is not a matter of individualism, but a process of adopting an organizational culture of growth and exploration. The stronger your team of Vikings, the more successful you will be at thriving in an era of change.

Thinking beyond your field is more than a catchy magazine article theme. We need to think beyond the traditional park and recreation field to find new opportunities and achieve excellence. If you want to take the best of business principles and apply them to your world, you need to study the best in the business world. I would strongly suggest reading Harvard Business Review to get a handle on what the leaders in management, marketing, and strategy are thinking about. For practical knowledge that will help the bottom line of your park agency, send your agency's best and brightest to NRPA's Revenue Development and Management School at Oglebay. This business school for park and recreation has been instilling entrepreneurism in park officials for over 45 years, with constantly updated course material.

Think about what Richard Louv and his book, *Last Child in the Woods*, did for outdoor/nature experiences. He changed the prevailing thinking on time spent in nature from a nice thing to do for some to a social imperative. As a result, nature programming and acquisition of open space have bloomed.

Think about new ways of positioning your park agency. If you are just considered the "fun" agency, you will be the first to be cut in economic hard times. But if your facilities and programs are a big reason tourists spend money in your community or why businesses locate there, you are no longer discretionary but have become essential.

These are examples of thinking beyond your field, looking for new markets and new worlds to explore. You can think like a Viking in looking for new revenue sources, new programming opportunities, new financing options, and new marketing methods. And, to thrive in an unsettled world, you need a strong team of Vikings to row that long boat to new opportunities.

(Reprinted with permission.)

Valhalla

Michael McCarty
Director of Parks and Recreation for the City of Fairfax, Virginia

From *Parks & Recreation Magazine*, October 2010, pp. 28–29

In the September issue of *Parks & Recreation*, Paul Gilbert, executive director of the Northern Virginia Regional Park Authority in Fairfax Station, Virginia, asked, "Are you a Viking or a farmer?"

The Viking, he wrote, seeks the adventures and risks that come with meeting challenges head on. The farmer is happy and content to manage his or her crops and maintain the land. The farmer sits back and lets change happen—or, in our field, allows budgets to get slashed and services reduced. It's this Viking mentality that creates change and opportunity. It's what allows people around us to see parks and recreation as an important service, not because we are a threat, but because we accomplish our goals and mission.

How can our profession be linked to these two cultures? Compare these two professions and cultures and see. As agencies begin to determine their make-up, I anticipate many will answer that we are farmers with little chance or desire to be Vikings.

The concept of linking the modern organization—whether it's a parks and recreation organization or corporation— to a Viking or farmer culture has been explored many times, most recently in an article in the March issue of the *Harvard Business Review* entitled, "Managers must make sure their teams are not avoiding critical conversations." The article asks a similar question to the one posed by Mr. Gilbert. The response links 21st century organizations to the culture of Vikings and farmers. Both articles should have us thinking and acting on many fronts, preparing for battle—less for simple survival than for a future Viking-like culture. The articles prompt many questions: "Who are the Vikings and farmers in our agencies?" "Am I a Viking or a farmer?" "Do we need Vikings and farmers, and if so, what should we do with the Vikings and farmers?" "How do you find and keep Vikings?" "What strategies can we focus on to be a Viking culture?"

While many other questions and discussions could be raised from such an interesting topic, let's concentrate on one area: identifying strategies to create a Viking culture in a parks and recreation setting.

The world of the Viking was a hostile and ever-changing place—just the climate to motivate him to be entrepreneurial and seek out better lives and land. They attacked many places controlled by nobles whose followers were fearful of change and interested only in survival. In most cases, it made for easy conquest. The followers had no incentive to fight, nor would they benefit greatly from the nobles. The Viking, on the other hand, shared in a common goal for which all would benefit equally in conquest.

Mr. Gilbert refers to the farmer as a manager. Today, many of our parks and recreation agencies are full of managers—or farmers—fearful of change. Fear of change can extend to such situations as adding new responsibilities to current workloads; taking another position in another agency and thus relocating families; or simply trying something new that may fail. The warrior culture of the Viking had vision, collective goals, and a team committed to these goals. They were rewarded with land and riches for achieving their goals. This doesn't sound much different from what we all want in our agencies, although instead of land and riches, it's resources, salary increases, and recognition we seek.

We need Viking leaders in our organizations seeking out new opportunities to achieve goals and realize visions. It's not simply about new programs or sources of revenue. It's also about recruiting people to your cause, selling the vision to your team of warriors and to the nobles in your world—the decision makers who provide the funding and support to achieve your vision.

As I researched more of the Viking and Norse culture, I came across a theory of leadership based on the Viking or Norse Valhalla—Odin's celestial hall where the souls of great warriors reside in the afterlife. The theory presented by Tom Geddie in his article titled "Tales of Viking Glory: Live the V.A.L.H.A.L.L.A. Theory of Leadership for Communicators" presents eight elements common to mighty warriors:

- **Values.** Trust and common purpose must be built on common values. These values guide us and help us to make decisions in our work and lives.
- **Assert yourself.** Take action to understand what's going on in your organization. Only when you understand how your agency functions and is being perceived by others can you begin to make decisions on the values you have established.
- **Let go of the little stuff.** Leadership is not about power; it's about letting the talents of others grow. Don't focus on the small things and micromanage. Find ways to build an entrepreneurial culture that celebrates change, failure, and ultimately success.
- **Holistic.** The holistic approach requires everyone in our organizations to understand how their actions affect the entire organization, whether it's the parks laborer taking a nap in the city vehicle or the management staff not being able to articulate the true benefits and economic impact to our political decision makers.
- **Aid and abet.** To attain a holistic culture and one that fosters the entrepreneurial sense, assist your employees in accomplishing their goals. Mentor and coach the employees, building up confidence and helping them to recognize their strengths and use their talents.
- **Listen and learn.** Listen to your staff, customers, and decision makers. Learn from what they are saying or not saying. You need to gain insight from many different sources and through many different means. Create

measurements to track results from your feedback and use those metrics to prove or improve your effectiveness.

Lead. In order to be a leader, you have to lead. The old saying, "Lead by example" rings true. Everyone around your organization needs to see that you lead like a Viking. That you, in fact, create opportunities for them to act as Vikings themselves.

Avid. We all need to be passionate advocates for the vision or the cause. We need to believe in what we do. Although my explanation of the elements of Valhalla is adapted for the purposes of this article, they stay true to the concepts presented by Tom Geddie. The Viking mentality is one way to navigate these turbulent waters. We need to recognize the opportunity we have to deliver on our mission and achieve a vision that parks and recreation are truly essential to everyone in our community. (*Reprinted with permission.*)

A Crisis of Knowledge

Tom Lovell

Administrator of Lee's Summit Parks & Recreation, Lee's Summmit, Missouri

From *Parks & Recreation Magazine*, January 2011, pp. 28–29

Until we educate our communities on the essential nature of parks and recreation, we will be sentenced to a downward spiral of declining resources and support.

As I read the articles by Paul Gilbert and Mike McCarty in the September and October issues of *Parks & Recreation*, it was refreshing to see more practitioner dialogue in our publication. It is crucial that our practitioners engage in the discussions that will shape our future.

To the point of the two articles, we are a profession under a silent siege as the economy forces our elected officials to make decisions that are rarely based on the long- or short-term cost-benefit analysis of competing interests. This is, however, through no fault of the elected officials. The magnitude of their ignorance is only rivaled by our own. My good friend and comrade in arms on this subject, Barry Weiss, characterizes it best with his quote of Albert Einstein: "Insanity is doing the same thing over and over but expecting a different result." I mean no disrespect, but until we fundamentally change our model of "doing business" to garner resources at all levels of government to serve all people, we will always be at the end of the line, or maybe not in line at all.

My read of the two articles was enjoyable, though it seemed like "back to the future." Those of us who experienced the last few economic downturns felt the same pressures as today. Our response, as suggested by the authors, is the same: do more with less and be more aggressive and entrepreneurial in our approach to service delivery. And we are.

A strong current runs through our profession now that is representative of a business approach to our development and management of facilities and services. This is a critical aspect of our operations today and in the competitive marketplace of parks and recreation it is essential to maintaining our market share.

But there is another critical aspect of our services that entails access. All of our citizens, regardless of economic status or physical/mental ability, deserve access to these services and facilities. It becomes even more important that resources can be obtained that ensure this access by all. The argument/data for this must be strong enough that it, too, becomes a part of the business model that we use to obtain our resources.

But it is not working for the long term. Some of us are not being asked to do more with less but to do less with less. An article in the September 2010 issue of *Governing* magazine, "Doing Less with Less," chronicles a troubling situation in Colorado Springs, where an excellent parks and recreation system operated as a best practice system is being decimated. This is not a situation of staff working harder or being more entrepreneurial— it is ignorance on the part of the citizens and elected officials in their decision making. To counter such situations, we must immediately begin repositioning our field in terms of the tangible values and benefits of a strong parks and recreation system.

As the late accreditation expert Betty van der Smissen so aptly put it several years ago during my department's first accreditation review, "We must become the teachers and interpreters of the values and benefits of what we do or we will perish." This is not, as last fall's column on Viking strategies suggested, just a matter of being more entrepreneurial or more aggressive in the market place. It is simply about the people we serve and the people they elect having a solid understanding of the compelling "tangible values and benefits" provided by a strong parks and recreation system.

We should all feel a sense of urgency to address this crisis. We are the only ones to fix it. Our students should graduate knowing hundreds of metric-based benefits to make the case for essentiality.

Our own practitioners should know hundreds of metric-based benefits to citizens should know these benefits, and of course our elected officials should know them. Whose fault is it that we have this problem? As Pogo said years ago, "I have met the enemy and he is us."

I hope that NRPA is paying attention and developing (or causing to be developed) the training tools necessary to reposition our profession. I am not talking about just rebranding, increased lobbying efforts, more national partnerships, or more presentations. We need to document the outcomes of our services and how we make people's lives better. We need these hundreds of metric-based benefits and the formulas to apply them to our own communities. We need ready-to-use editorials, presentations, social media pieces, and strategies to utilize them. Simply, we need major repositioning tools that can be applied at the local level. We need practitioners to become educators and interpreters.

We need citizens who understand the metric-based value of short- and longterm fixes for health care, environmental sustainability, economic activity, and community development that a strong parks and recreation system can provide a community.

So, our new mantra should be: "I have met the solution and it is us."

(Reprinted with permission.)

Secrets of Farmers and Vikings

Randolph P. Ferris
APIFOG Management and Consulting

From *Parks & Recreation Magazine*, April 2011, p. 26

It's All About Cross-Training and Prioritizing Direct-Service

I have enjoyed the forum published in the September and October 2010 "Kiosk" section of *Parks & Recreation*. Comparing parks and recreation agencies to Vikings and farmers brings a new light to our situations.

Both articles, and those that followed in subsequent months, have overlooked one of the main reasons both farmer- and Viking-style management structures were and are successful: Everyone pitches in. All members of the organization are direct-service providers, and all are cross-trained to replace other members of their team should they not be available. If one Viking falls in battle, no extensive search for a replacement is necessary. Another Viking does the job. Farmers have long epitomized the "jack of all trades, master of none" stereotype, where all members of the team can do whatever is needed at any given time.

Parks and recreation agencies have expanded their support and specialist classifications for a variety of reasons over the years; some by mandate by their governmental structure to increase oversight and administrative compliance, others for other reasons. This has resulted in large headquarters staff levels and new departments that oversee functions such as revenue collection and tracking patron usage.

While these endeavors certainly have value and merit, they are not direct-service providers. Taxpayers hear that more money is needed to fix park facilities and build more playgrounds. They accept the cost of the playground, but are mostly unaware of the landscape architect and the purchasing contract specialist and the tract to construct the playground on land the agency already owns. Some additional education of our patrons can help to explain why these things cost more when governments do them, but taxpayers still may refuse to pay the higher prices.

If cuts are to be made, then retention priorities need to focus on direct-service providers. Viking-type scenarios worked because of cross-training and all hands doing all things. Farmers who succeed do so by pushing resources into outcomes, not lateral functions. Yes, some tracking and documenting is needed, but not by exclusive specialists. Our own country's U.S. Army Special Forces, the Green Berets, use a similar hierarchy when mobilizing. Team function responsibilities are assigned to specific members, but each member must cross-train in two other team functions, so that if needed, all services are delivered even if team members are lost or incapacitated.

"Silo" effects of sections within a department performing similar functions, or employing staff as specialists who represent the function of another section of a department, are also large consumers of resources. These are often either overlooked as "the way things have always been," or defended by middle management, which is reluctant to give up the luxury of that exclusive asset in lieu of returning to the dependence on the original section performing their function for them. Common examples are human resources specialists assigned to larger sections of departments, even though a separate human resources section exists to perform these tasks. Other functions often duplicated are marketing/communications, safety/security, and information technology.

My point boils down to one simple phrase: When cutting department resources becomes unavoidable, the priorities must go to keeping the direct-service providers who do the job that the department was created to perform in the first place. (*Reprinted with permission.*)

Organizational Structure

How Does the Way an Organization is Structured Affect How It Performs?

One of the key differences between an efficient and nimble organization and an inefficient and bureaucratic one is the organizational structure. The reason for this is that structure has a great effect on the flow of information and the ability of different areas of the organization to work with each other, as well as how decisions are made. Structure also has a great effect on the ability to change and adapt, in other words, the organization's *flexibility*.

The way an organization is structured is very much like the way a machine is built. It has a lot to do with how well it will run. The first Wright Flyer and a modern jet fighter are both machines built for flight, but the way they are built has everything to do with how they perform. The 1903 Wright Flyer could fly less than 1,000 feet at some unknown but slow speed, and an F-16 can fly over 2,000 miles and reach speeds of Mach 2. The difference lies in how they are built. Often we don't think much about how organizations are made; however, structure greatly affects how organizations perform, just as with machines.

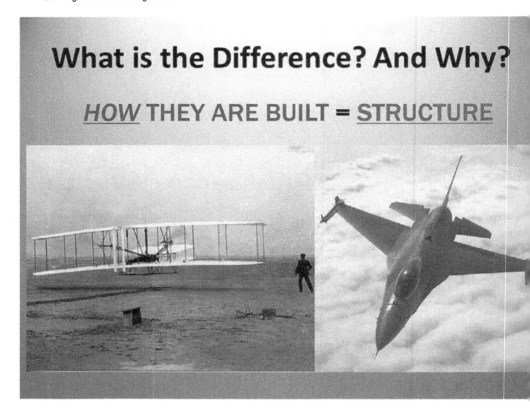

You can generally view an organizational structure most clearly on an organizational chart. Such charts show the lines of authority from the governance board (city or county council/board or other governance body) to the CEO position of the organization (city or county manager/executive/director), to the departments and subunits (divisions) within the department. Ideally, an organizational chart should indicate exactly who everyone reports to in the organization.

The two polar opposites in organizational structure are hierarchical vs. flat (see Figures 2.1 and 2.2). In the hierarchical structure, there are many layers in the organization, while in a perfectly flat organization, there

Be intentional about how the agency is structured,

it will directly affect performance.

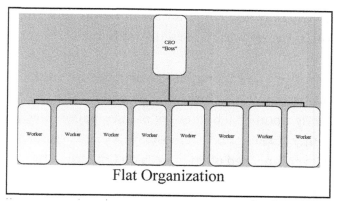

Figure 2.1. Flat Organizational Chart

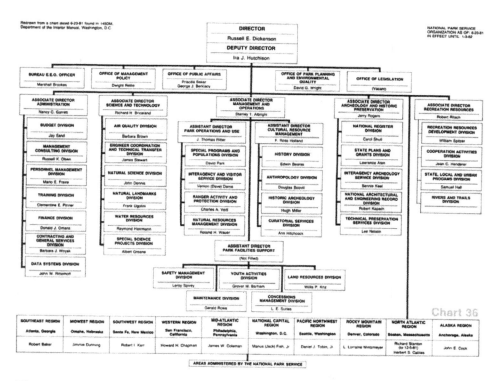

Figure 2.2. Hierarchical Organizational Chart

would be essentially two levels, one for the "boss" and one for everyone else, who would all be equals on the organizational chart. While flatter organizations are more flexible than extremely hierarchical ones, the idea of a truly flat organization can only really work in a very small group of not much more than 10. Beyond that level, some structured layers will likely be necessary. Generally, the larger an organization gets, the more levels are needed within the organization chart just to maintain supervision accountability.

The growth in organizational layers happens to most organizations over time, and particularly in large organizations. The challenge is each additional layer is a potential bottleneck of information flow and decision making. The other challenge is that most layers in an organization develop incrementally over time, and often there is no time when the overall structure is examined for efficiency. One of the dynamics that happens is that the people in the organizations assume that the structure that has evolved is really the only way to organize things, and that you need all those people in those positions. In truth, other and more efficient structures could most likely be used; they would just require change, which is stressful for many.

There is also the dynamic of social status that is attached to how many people and how large a budget a manager has authority over. The human desire for status that drives managers to have larger staffs and bigger budgets is the same impulse that leads to organizational fiefdoms.

Obstacles to creating agencies and departments that are more flexible, efficient, and customer-focused can be seen below (Golembiewski, 1985):

- Higher level executives avoid delegating authority
- Government = procedural regularity and caution
- Role of professional managers is poorly developed compared to business

Executives who are unwilling or unable to delegate authority are an example of the potential bottleneck of both information flow and decision making that can result from too many levels in an organization.

The issue of too many rules and regulations and the generally slow-moving cautious nature of many governmental organizations is an issue of organizational life cycle. As organizations become increasingly bureaucratic, it is a sign of organizational decline. There is a need for rules in some parts of an organization, particularly to assure financial accountability. But in general, rules should only be adopted when truly needed. Excess regulations kill the flexibility, creativity, and initiative that are key to an entrepreneurial approach in parks and recreation.

In the 1980s and 1990s, there was a great deal of thought that organizational silos were the way to promote efficiency (Figures 2.3 and 2.4). The thought was to create organizations within organizations so better communication and information flow within the smaller group might be fostered. The unintended consequence was that these insulated groups did not work that well together as a whole. The other consequence was that locking talent and resources down within a sub-group meant that those resources were not available to be deployed where they were needed in a changing environment. Silos did not work well in a static environment, and they are even less effective in a dynamic environment where flexibility is at a premium.

So What Is the Best Organizational Structure?

There is no one structure that is ideal for every organization, but the principles that can guide effective organization are the following.

Form Follows Function

In both side bar examples, you can see that structure affects how individuals and groups within an organization see their role, and such perceptions have profound effects on performance. If you want to build an organization where responsibility for financial performance or other elements is shared, then do not isolate those roles, or others will not see it as their job. Instead of having some subgroup of operations under an enterprise fund (entrepreneurial) and some under general fund (taxpayer support), maybe a larger portion of the agency is shifted under the enterprise fund to send a message to everyone that revenue recovery and efficient operations are important across the board.

Figure 2.3. Silos Limit Flexibility

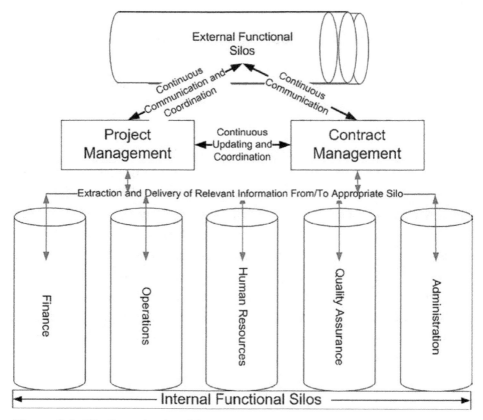

Figure 2.4. Silo Organizational Structure

Form Follows Function
How Structure Affects Performance

A community nonprofit board had a fund-raising committee. After a while, this committee that embodied the most difficult task of any nonprofit board had dwindled in numbers of board members interested in serving on it. Other board members focused on the fun community mission elements and assumed the job of raising funds was for the few on the fund raising committee.

The solution was to eliminate the committee and reinforce that fund raising was the job of the entire board and make it a focus of every board meeting. The result of the structural change was that the board raised more funds and better understood that this difficult role was a critical part of everyone's responsibility.

Nimble Flexibility

In a changing environment, there is a need to be able to redeploy your resources in new ways. Maybe that means an "all hands on deck" special event or having staff with special skills work for some period of time at a different site than they usually do, under a different supervisory structure. Whatever the needs are, the organization must have the flexibility to adjust. This means avoiding rigid silos and fiefdoms and trying to keep the structure as flat and flexible as necessary. Using cross-functional teams as often as possible builds communication across organizational lines and can ease realignment when it is needed.

Keep Overhead Low

If one of the goals is to reduce the need for as much taxpayer support, one of the strategies is to try to minimize the amount of the organization that is not directly providing services to the customers. Some overhead is necessary; after all, functions such as budgeting, finance, human resources, planning and development, and organizational leadership are necessary, but these functions should be thought out and organized to be effectively done with no more people than necessary. One tactic for reducing overhead and just operating at maximum efficiency is never filling a vacant position just because it is in the budget and someone used to do that job. With every vacancy, ask the key people in that area to think about how the needed jobs could be done. Can you outsource some functions, change the process for how things are done, or otherwise do that function more efficiently? Much of why organizations grow over time is because these tough questions are not regularly asked, and the first and easiest answer to many questions is to hire a new person to do whatever function needs to be done. Hiring someone new is the first and easiest answer, but the easy answers often get in the way of the best ones.

In-Source Revenue and Out-Source Expense

Which functions do you want to handle in house, and which ones you want to outsource? In general, it is better to look at in-sourcing areas that bring in significant revenue. Doing so can mean that the agency will capture a larger share of the net return than they would if they contracted out key money-making activities. On the other side, if there are expense areas where you do not do enough of that kind of work to effectively utilize people and equipment, it is a great candidate for contracting out.

The good news is that planned organization development changes can be just as successful in the public sector as they are in the private sector. A meta-analytic comparison of 47 organizational development initiatives in the 20th century showed strong levels of success in both sectors for changes focused on improving efficiencies of organizations (Robertson & Seneviratne, 1995). One of the challenges in making organizational change successful is in the ability to measure success. Many private sector organization have more obvious measurements of success, which makes it easier to design and track organizational changes. Public sector organizations must do this too; it just might take more thought to determine the key measurable results that will be tracked and measured against.

An Example of Successful Outsourcing

Orange County Park District in California operates a number of beach parks and associated beach parking areas. It started exploring outsource parking services in 2005 as it researched alternatives to the task of park rangers collecting revenue at the pay and display machines and recommend either a contract service or another option.

Prior to deciding on outsourcing the entire operation, OC Parks considered upgrading the parking equipment on its own. After considering multiple options, OC Parks decided to outsource the entire parking management operation. The decision was based on the following factors:

Core Business Functions

OC Parks, as one of the premier park systems in the nation, is committed to having a customer-centric approach toward recreation, outreach programs, and stewardship. Managing parking operations with field resources is not part of its core business functions.

Resource Utilization

Parking operations under OC Parks was performed by park rangers, maintenance staff, office technicians, and park attendants. Park rangers, maintenance staff, and office technicians are full-time OC Parks employees. Park attendants were extra help, part-time employees. Given the amount of time that OC Parks employees (especially park rangers) spent on parking-related activities, it was not a good utilization of full-time staff resources.

Productivity

A significant amount of employee time was spent in coordinating multiple vendors to do regular maintenance and equipment repair related to parking pay and display machines.

Loss of Revenue

The pay and display machines were in need of repair and would frequently become out of order, during which time OC Parks would not collect parking revenue. Also, the equipment was incapable of accepting larger bills or credit/debit cards, which meant a loss of potential revenue.

Cost Avoidance

A significant amount of investment was needed to upgrade the pay and display machines. OC Parks realized that by outsourcing the parking program, those costs would be borne by the company who presented the most competitive bid.

Risk Transfer

OC Parks employees were responsible for retrieving, counting, and coordinating the deposit of parking-related revenue to the bank. Managing these large sums of money posed a risk to employees. OC Parks would be able to transfer that risk by outsourcing parking operations to an outside company.

After a competitive bidding process, Parking Concepts, Inc. began managing the parking at the beach and wilderness facilities and Peters Canyon Regional Park (pay and display parking facilities) in November 2008. After one year of management, gross revenue increased 20% compared to the previous year.

PCi began managing the parking at nine additional regional parks in November 2009. After one year of management, gross revenue at those nine facilities increased 15% compared to the previous year.

During the final 12-month period (November 2007 to October 2008) of OC Parks managing parking at beach, wilderness, and regional parks, annual net income to OC Parks was $1,620,247. During PCi's first 12-month period (November 2009 to October 2010) of managing parking at beach, wilderness, and regional parks, annual net income to OC Parks increased to $1,798,949 (11% increase).

Since PCi began managing parking, OC Parks has realized increased gross revenue, increased net income, new and upgraded pay and display machines, upgraded software, and reduced pay and display machine downtime. In addition, field personnel are able to focus on their core responsibilities.

One reason this is a great example of outsourcing is that OC Parks determined early on that running the parking operations was not central to its mission and skill set. Outsourcing is a great idea of functions that others can do more efficiently. In this case, PCi was a company that specialized in parking lot operations, they used the best equipment, and their staff was focused solely on this portion of the operations.

Mission and Momentum

Why Does the Organization Exist, and What Is the Key to Achieving Great Results?

Journalism students are taught that the key elements of any story are the following:

- Who?
- What?
- Where?
- When?
- Why?
- How?

If you can answer all of these questions, you know the full story. For a parks, recreation, or tourism organization, the "who" question may be answered in the organizational beginnings. Was a new department of a city or county formed at some time in the past to deal with these community needs? Was a park district or authority authorized by the state legislature? Was a nonprofit corporation set up to promote tourism or offer recreational services?

The "what" question is answered in the day-to-day activities of the group, and the "where" addresses the geographical service area. The "when" is the lifetime of the organization. The "how" question is best answered with a good strategic plan, which we will look at in the next chapter.

speaks to mission or vision. This is the most important question to know the answer to. If you know why, you know the core issue that drives all the others. Because of this, mission is important to communicate to employees, elected officials, and the general public why an organization exists and what it hopes to accomplish in the future. Occasionally, the "why" is expressed in the mission statement. Too often, the mission statement lacks the core that it needs. At its best, a mission statement is short, memorable, and aspirational. If done well, a good mission statement can be the bedrock that a winning strategic plan can be built on. It can also be a yardstick that any decision of the organization has been measured against. A good mission statement can help the organization make principled decisions about many issues and can help the organization know when to say "yes" to an idea that advances its mission, and more importantly, "no" when a decision is not consistent with the mission.

Many directors of local park and recreation departments complain about the frequent political pressure to offer new services without additional resources or to favor a local athletic group because the group has lobbied local elected officials. Without a clear mission and preferably a good strategic plan to achieve the mission, it is too easy to be blown by the political winds without having a good argument for why a given service or favor to a user group should not be done. In this way, a good mission statement can be the first step in having a more principled and professional measure for what the agency should be doing. Public park and recreation agencies all provide various functions to serve community needs that do not generate revenue. These services enhance the community in various ways but are expensive. A good mission statement that can be used as a measuring stick to see if a given proposal is worth taking on is essential. Without it, the agency can become a collection of well-intentioned programs without funding. With a mission statement as a way to measure if a program fits the organization, better decisions can be made.

Many agencies have a cost-recovery policy that goes a step further. Such a policy is very specific about what kinds of programs can "lose money" and what types of programs need to recover 100% or greater of their direct costs. So a program that would serve underprivileged youth, such as midnight basketball, might be all or largely paid for by tax dollars, while a program that benefits an individual or small group, such as a personal trainer at a gym, would need to cover 100% or more of its full costs.

There are many examples of good agencies that do not have articulated mission statements or have ones that are too much "all things to all people" to be useful. Often, the mission of the organization is understood and ingrained in institutional knowledge. Such embedded institutional missions can serve an agency for years, but eventually the institutional knowledge can be lost when people leave, or tested if there is significant political pressure brought to bear without a formal mission to measure against.

Some Good Examples

Phoenix Police Department

"To Ensure the Safety and Security for Each Person in our Community"

Parks and Recreation Department, Denver, Colorado

"As stewards of Denver's legacy, the Department of Parks and Recreation is dedicated to customer satisfaction and enhancing lives by providing innovative programs and safe, beautiful, sustainable places."

Parks and Recreation Department, Miami, Florida

"To provide state-of-the-art park facilities and offer leisure, educational, cultural, and physical activities to the residents and visitors of our community, while enhancing their quality of life and inspiring personal growth, self-esteem, pride, and respect for the urban environment."

A Mission Without Much Mission

Municipal Services, City of Lowell, Arkansas

"The mission of the Municipal Services Department evolves around the responsibility of planning, providing, and maintaining the city's facilities, and recreation activities."

The reason the mission statement from the City of Lowell is lacking is because it is purely descriptive of what they are doing without addressing the central purpose of a mission, which is to express why the agency is engaged in its activities. Remember the mission is to answer the *why* question, not the *what* question.

A mission statement should also be short for a number of reasons. First, the mission should be something that most people in the organization could either recite or paraphrase. It should be very visible. Put it on the web page, post it on the walls inside the buildings and most used public places of the agency, and include it on most of the brochures and other print materials of the organization.

The second reason it should be short is that it shows clarity of purpose. A long mission statement might be the result of an organization that is not clear about who they are and what they want to become. A long statement might mean the organization needs to do more work and consensus building around its mission.

While it is optimal for the why question to be clearly stated in the mission statement; if it is not (and many are not), still push yourself to answer that question. If you can express this core meaning for what you are doing, it will help in building your team and achieving your goals.

Strategic Planning

How Do You Drive Organizational Growth and Achieve the Vision?

Now that you have a compelling and noble mission statement, how do you take the organization from where it is today to where it could be in the future? The answer is with a strategic plan. This is the most important document in the organization. That is worth repeating: *This is the most important document in the organization!*

Whether riding a bike, driving a car, or skiing down a mountain, you will go wherever you are looking. So where you put your focus is an issue of tremendous and profound importance. And where do most of us put most of our attention and focus? On day-to-day tasks, with 50 pending e-mails in the in-box, five phone messages to return, a big event coming

Focus on where you want to go . . .

up in a few days, and several people needing to talk to you, it is hard not to focus on the very real needs of today. The problem is that tomorrow and the day after that and the day after that will be very similar. And if you only focus on the tasks of today, you will never take the steps needed to build a stronger organization and a brighter future. Most of us spend so little time thinking about the future and what small steps can be taken now that will create that brighter future, that many people are uncomfortable thinking and working on long-term planning. But without a strategic plan and good attention to it, the future will look much like today. Remember, you will go where you are focusing. In a static environment, that might have been okay, but in a changing dynamic environment, strategic planning is more important than ever before.

The timing of a strategic plan is usually between 3 to 10 years, with the most common goal being a 5-year plan. Five years is a great time horizon, because it pushes you out of the kind of annual planning that most organizations do a lot of with their budgets. And yet it is not so futuristic that it is unconnected with actions you will take in the next few years. Often, when you set a long-term goal, it is hard to see how you will achieve it, because so many of us live day to day. What happens with a good strategic plan is that if the first few steps are achieved, the resources of the organization will be stronger, and the next few steps will be more achievable. It is like climbing to a new plateau or vantage point, all of a sudden the view becomes totally different, and the realm of possibilities is expanded. And at every new plateau, the view will expand again. Without a strategic plan, you will always be at the same level. The strategic plan does not need to be a trail map to the top of the mountain, just one to get you to the next level or two. Once you arrive at those new levels, the plan can be updated to take you up the mountains a few more levels.

Since most people are not used to thinking about the future and how to grow resources, a great challenge of strategic planning is to move past the day to day. Since staff members are the ones most engaged in the day-to-day challenges of operating the organization, a good way to start a strategic planning process is with a staff retreat that is a brainstorming session. Push everyone to think of a 3- to 5-year horizon, but allow all input to be recorded. If a staff member is concerned about a certain challenge today, it will be hard to move past it to future thinking until the current challenge is recorded. These current challenges may give you a great list of near-term projects to tackle, but use a strict filter on what goes into the strategic plan. By honoring today's issues, you will be able to set them aside for a while and begin to think long term.

A good strategic plan provide the North Star for everyone in your organization to navigate by.

It provides the directions and steps that will lead to a brighter future.

What Goes in the Plan

The items that make it into the long-term strategic plan should not be the list of short-term issues that come up first in many brainstorming sessions. The goal of a strategic plan is not to record every action that will be done in the next few years. Instead, the challenge is to identify the key steps that need to be taken to move the organization to the new higher plateau. These are the few key steps that will grow the capacity of the organization and achieve the mission in a better way. A short list of major initiatives also gives the organization the flexibility it needs to deal with changing circumstances. If you attempted to record everything, or many things, that should be done in the next five years, you would have little opportunity to take advantage of new unforeseen opportunities or challenges.

While the longer initial brainstorming list is most likely very different from the final strategic plan, it is vitally necessary. First, good ideas will come from brainstorming, some for shorter term initiatives and some that may lead to strategic planning action items. Secondly, it is vitally important that there is buy-in throughout the organization if you are going to be successful with implementation. Buy-in does not mean that every idea makes it into the final plan, but rather that every idea is heard and considered, and the key ones that help the organization reach a higher level make it into the plan.

Plan Development Process

While staff buy-in is vital for long-term success, strategic planning is central to good governance. And the role of governance is that of the governing body, whether it is a city council, board of directors, county board, etc. These elected or appointed officials who make up the governance board must be the ones to formally adopt the strategic plan as their own. They must also be fully invested that the strategic plan is the blueprint for strategic actions over the next few years. This should be the document on which the progress of the organization is measured. Just as staff needs time to brainstorm in the strategic planning process, so does the governance board. This may mean a strategic planning retreat for the governance board would be a good thing to follow the initial staff retreat. The governance board needs to appreciate the vital importance of staff buy-in to the plan, and the staff needs to understand that the final plan is a product of the governance board. So it needs to be a collaborative effort with the governance board having the final say.

Most strategic plans take months to develop with multiple input sessions for different groups including staff, board, and public stakeholder groups. Many organizations use consultants to help facilitate the development of a strategic plan. If using a consultant, make sure that the end result is an authentic plan for your organization and not just a worked-over plan that was done for the last few organizations the consultant worked for. The consultant's role should be more of process facilitator and less of plan writer.

All of this process takes time, and it is time well spent. With a strategic plan, buy-in is essential if it is going to do more than adorn a shelf. And making a short and clearly stated strategic plan that encompasses the important strategic steps and measurable results will take some time to write. Mark Twain once wrote: "I would have written a shorter letter, but I did not have the time." As funny as this quote sounds, it does take more time to write a piece that is tight and to the point; a long-winded strategic plan with too many details is not the goal. The goal is a high-level outline of game-changing steps that will lead to a brighter future.

Key Tools to Be Used in Developing a Strategic Plan

Mission

Always keep the mission front and center in any discussion of the future.

Vision Statement

To supplement the mission statement, sometimes it is useful to start at the end and come up with a narrative statement about what your organization could look like by the end of the strategic planning period. How will it be serving the community and benefiting the world? How will its people, places, and finances be stronger?

Strengths, Weaknesses, Opportunities and Threats (SWOT)

Assessing how your organization, facilities, or programs stack up in each of these four categories can give you a great picture of where you are within your marketplace. Strengths and weaknesses assess your internal abilities, and opportunities and threats focus on how you fit into the external world (Figure 4.1). The internal vs. external nature of these questions is often lost, as people just look at the four words and not what they are about.

Internal questions. The internally focused questions about strengths and weaknesses are the ones that will lead to issues of organizational de-

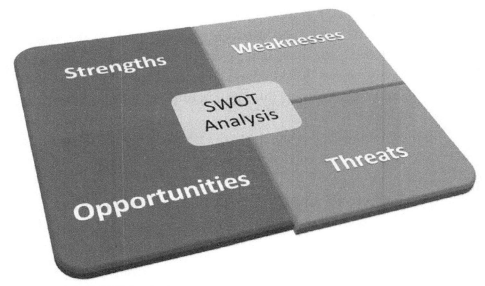

Figure 4.1. SWOT Analysis

velopment. And, most important in these two areas is a focus on building on the unique strengths your group has. You can only make marginal improvements focusing on the negative issue of weaknesses, but a focus on strengths can unleash the amazing and untapped potential of your organization. Focusing on developing your internal potential is also a great process, because it is an area where you can make the greatest difference.

External questions. External awareness is very important. Just like with the internal questions, a focus on the positive dynamic of opportunity is going to be much more productive than too much time spent on threats. The reason for this is control and influence. You have very little control and influence over the potential external threats in life. They often just consume energy in unproductive ways. The area where you can have influence is looking at unique external opportunities and taking advantage of them. What changes in the market or your customers' desires align with your strengths in a way where you can take advantage of the opportunity?

Just like the perception test in the earlier sidebar, you will only see what you are looking for. So while the SWOT gives you a great overall situational awareness, you need to focus your attention on the strengths and opportunities where you can take action and make positive change. Too much focus on weaknesses and threats can lead to negative cycles. The focus on threats is both unlimited in the number of bad things that could potentially happen, and unempowering in that there is generally little that can be done about all the potentially bad yet unlikely things that could happen. So be aware of your full situation, but focus your time and efforts on the positive things that are within your realm of influence.

Though assessing all four factors is important to understand where you are in the marketplace, the strategic plan should also be focused on the strengths and opportunities. Remember that you will go where you are focused. So focusing most of your attention on the negative aspects of weaknesses and threats will not make a stronger, better organization. Only by focusing on developing strengths and identifying and using opportunities to their best advantage will growth and development come.

Needs assessment. This kind of assessment is usually in the form of a public opinion poll showing what type of facilities and programs are most needed and valued by the public. Often, the results of these types of polls are counterintuitive to parks and recreation officials. Many go into such surveys with the assumptions that youth athletics will be number one because the athletic groups are so vocal. In most cases, a poll of the general public shows a much higher value for open space, trails, and more passive parkland. This can be an eye-opening experience.

Many park agencies look at national ratios of how many different kinds of facilities a community needs based on population. This is very much a "cookie-cutter" approach. Not every community is the same, and just because 20 years ago some consultant 1,000 miles away decided you need X number of soccer fields per 1,000 people does not mean that this ratio is right for your needs today. Too often these ratios drive agencies to spend all their resources on creating very standard park systems. On the down side, such a focus can choke out the resources to innovate the field and serve the public in new and dynamic ways.

Key Elements of a Successful Plan

Just as a mission statement needs clarity, so does a strategic plan. It should not be a long document that includes a lot of details. Every item included in the plan should be able to pass the following test questions: "If we achieve this goal, will it be a transformative step that makes us a stronger organization?" If you cannot easily answer "yes" to that question, it might be a good thing to do but should not be included in the strategic plan. Remember, this plan should take your organization to the next level, the next plateau on the climb up the mountain.

After you have your strategic or transformational steps, you need to think about how you can measure progress toward achieving these goals. Here again, do not attempt to list all potential outcomes, but think about which two or three key indicators could be used to measure success. Be specific on the measurable goals. Here are a few examples:

Land Acquisition Goal

Review eight potential projects that meet our land selection criteria over the next two years. Acquire at least one new property over the next two years.

Expand Your Entrepreneurial Expertise

Send 10 staff to NRPA Revenue Development and Management School over the next five years. Have each revenue school graduate conduct at least two in-house training sessions with other staff on elements that they have learned.

Increase Program Participation

Conduct an analysis of all programs over the last 10 years, and phase out any program that has lost 20% participation over that time period. Research current trends and do a one-year pilot program for two new programs with a goal of 120% cost recovery.

Implementation

Once the plan is adopted, the challenge is to make the implementation of the plan central to the organization. This should not be the task of one employee; it should be broadly integrated into the fabric of the agency.

A good way to start is to connect the annual budget with the strategic plan as closely as possible. Be explicit that different funding in the budget is there to implement certain sections of the plan. The performance of the director/CEO of the organization should be measured on the success of the plan. Ideally, individual performance goals should be tied to this plan for as many employees as possible. And the governance board should review progress on achieving the plan on a regular basis.

If there is no concerted effort to integrate the plan into both the budget and personnel review, it is likely that the best plan will not be well implemented because once the plan is adopted, all those day-to-day obligations will creep in and take attention away from achieving a better tomorrow. It is only by forcing regular attention to these long-term goals that the organization will advance to the next level.

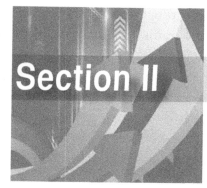

Section II

The Enterprise Approach

- Defining the Enterprise Approach
- Innovation
- Pricing
- Marketing
- Customer Service
- Partnering

Defining the Enterprise Approach

As we saw in the introduction, being entrepreneurial is about both taking "ownership" for our organization and being willing to take an active role in shaping the future through action. This means being willing to change and not remaining married to past practices.

Taking such a proactive approach will lead many to think about how to grow the resources of the organization so you can do a better job of achieving your mission. In the sidebar "Winning the Levy," you will see how Cleveland Metroparks was able to expand its funding by 50% by showing such value to their voters that they increased their taxing authority. This was a great success.

An alternative model of success is that of generating more funds through business-related activities. In the fields of parks, recreation, and tourism, one of the options available is to create programs and/or facilities that the public is willing to pay for. Such programs and facilities create enterprise operations. These business activities generate revenue that can help support and expand the organization.

The process of creating an enterprise operation is exciting because it only works well if you have created a product that some portion of the public wants enough to purchase. If this is done well it can grow the number of people you actively serve as your customer base finds the great offering you have created.

Creating successful enterprise operations requires innovation. Making enterprises both attractive to the customer and supportive of the organization requires an understanding of pricing. And attracting and retaining customers requires marketing and customer service. Being most cost effective in the delivery of these services may well require partnering. All of these skill sets are covered in the next chapters.

While the entrepreneurial approach is not entirely about raising money, it definitely includes bringing in more enterprise (self-generated) money. Expanding your funding base through enterprise activities will give your organization greater independence, strength, and the ability to offset other areas of your mission that do not support themselves.

A remarkable number of people think that for parks and recreation agencies to raise self-generated money means they must charge more for everything. This is really not the case. If you charge more than the customer is willing to pay, you will lose customers and fail to generate money.

For public parks, ideally access to the land should be free to all. Enterprise revenue can be generated by offering attractive, value-added services. When you add more value-added services (within reason) on public land, you create a win-win scenario where more people who are attracted by the amenities are introduced to the great open space. And at the same time, those coming to use the use the open space have more options available to them through the amenities.

When done right, an enterprise approach means you need to understand your customers and offer them products and services they value and are happy to pay for. Forget what you currently do, and think instead about who your current and potential customers are, what will make their lives better, and how you can offer that. If done well, you will raise more money, get more park visitors, and have a better relationship with your customers, because they will value and appreciate what you are offering. It is a win/win formula. And, while it may work differently in different communities, the fundamentals can be used in struggling communities as well as affluent ones.

The Secret Sauce
One Agency's Recipe for Success

The Northern Virginia Regional Park Authority (NVRPA), also known as NOVA Parks, grew its enterprise revenues by 83% between 2003 and 2013. And, more importantly, the growth was not in just one or two areas but across a wide range of enterprises creating a more diversified funding mix. This kind of growth is not the result of one great idea, but rather the result of an organizational culture that embraces challenges and looks for opportunities.

Where you put your focus and attention is where you will go. It is true in steering a bicycle and it is true in organizational management. Below are some recurring themes that help to define this focus:

Accountability

The "people factor" can never be underestimated. Having the right people in the right places and clear goals and objectives, so people are accountable for measurable results is key.

Customer Focus

Understanding who your core customer is and what they value has made a tremendous difference. In the last decade a focus to understanding who NVRPA's various target audiences are and working to build our products around their needs and desires has resulted in great improvements.

Unique Market Position

NVRPA's most unique and innovative facilities and programs are the ones that are most successful because they occupy a unique market position. In a world of "sameness" the more you can remain unique in your offerings, the stronger your long-term growth will be.

Return on Investment

Many of the great successes in revenue generation involve a strategic expansion or improvement on an existing facility. This is key for several reasons, one is that you are building on an existing customer base, which is easier than building an entirely new base, and two, by building on existing infrastructure you do not have the enormous capital costs of creating an entirely new facility, which creates a higher return on investment.

Winning the Levy

An Example of Winning Greater Tax Support

In November 2013, 70% of the voters in Greater Cleveland (Cuyahoga County and Hinckley Township) passed a 50% increase in the property tax that supports Cleveland Metroparks. So why did a rust-belt city like Cleveland have such an enthusiasm for a large tax increase over the next ten years? The answer is vision.

Selling a tax increase anywhere is not easy, but it can be done when the focus is less on the cost of the tax and more on the vision for the brighter future that the new levy will make possible. Brian Zimmerman, Chief Executive Officer of Cleveland Metroparks, was the primary spokesperson for the levy, and what he did was talk a lot about the future of a more vibrant and revitalized Cleveland that would come if the levy passed. While expanding trails and many new parks and amenities were part of the package, a great deal of focus was put on a new 455-acre lakefront park near downtown Cleveland that would enhance downtown. Selling this package of improvements, Zimmerman talked about the nuts and bolts of new parks, and stressed what it would mean to the area. "One of our goals is: What is it going to take to attract and retain high school and college graduates? We are really trying to contribute to that competitive advantage that I think Cleveland has versus another industrial city in the country," remarked Zimmerman.

Zimmerman continually emphasized Cleveland Metroparks and the importance of its nearly 23,000 acres of park lands and its diverse facilities. Importantly, he painted a picture of the better community that Cleveland could be with more for young people to do with an expanded and well-run park system. He addressed the real issues that people in older cities face. How do cities retain younger residents who are looking for a quality lifestyle and opportunities? How do city leaders make a downtown a more attractive place for major employers to locate? How do they generate more money from tourism to help improve schools and provide other needed services? All of these issues and more can be addressed with world class park systems. Park systems can learn from Cleveland and sell the vision for the future.

Business Plans
Creating the Plan for Enterprise Success

Many other plans have been discussed in this book: strategic plans, marketing plans, SWOT analysis, and others. Most of these are pieces that would feed into a good business plan. The purpose of a business plan is to completely examine and chart a plan for a specific enterprise or line  of business. Most organizations do many different things, and would be well served to have a business plan for each of those activities or enterprises.

Traditionally the purpose of a business plan was to help a new company figure out how they are going to operate and communicate their plans to funding sources, like banks, that might lend money to start the enterprise. In the public sector, a good business plan could help sell a new enterprise or facility to a city or county government.

For nearly 50 years, the Revenue Development and Management School at Oglebay WVA has been training professional in the parks and recreation field about best business practices. The completion of the two-year program has teams working together to put together a business plan for a new or expanding program or facility. After completing the plan, the students present their well-researched vision to a mock city council for approval.

This is great training for many reasons. First, it pulls together all that they have learned in the two-year program. And second, it exposes them to the very real experience of presenting a big plan to a group of elected official for approval. Elements of the business plan include the following:

- Executive summary
- Agency description
- Industry analysis
- Target market
- Competition
- Marketing plan
- Operations
- Management team
- Long-range plan
- Financial plan

Students also need to be able to work together in teams and be able to give an oral presentation in a time-limited environment. These are all skills for success in any professional field.

Innovation

How to Create New Markets and Distinguish Your Organization from the Competition

Going back to the analogy of the Viking or the farmer, the farmer focuses on his fields and manages his existing resources, while the Viking looks to the horizon to new opportunities and resources. For decades, the parks and recreation field has been a farmer's world, where competent managers did the best with the resources they were handed. In many cases, those resources were budgets funded largely with tax dollars. In the new era, agencies need to look to internally generated funds to operate and grow. This shift requires a Viking perspective, and that is where innovation comes in.

In its simplest form, innovation is a creative process. Whether it is coming up with an entirely new market or just improving a process or program, it all falls under the category of innovation. With many shifts happening in how people recreate and how they

"I'll be happy to give you innovative thinking. What are the guidelines?"

"There is no reason for any individual
to have a computer in the home."
Ken Olson
President of Digital Equipment Corp., 1977

"We don't like their sound.
Groups of guitars are on the way out."
Decca Recording Company Executive
after hearing the Beatles in 1962

"With over 50 foreign cars already on
sale here, the Japanese auto industry
isn't likely to carve out a big slice of
the U.S. market for itself."
Business Week, 1968

Sometimes the "Experts" Do Not See the Change that is about to Transform that Field.

get their information, we need parks, recreation, and tourism destinations to change with the population we service. There is a great deal of room for advancement in this area, considering how many parks and programs look much the same as they did years ago.

What concerns many people when the subject of innovation is brought up is that many believe it relies on a high level of innate (God-given) creative talent. While some people are more creative than others, with the tools and methods in this chapter, any group can start the process of innovating.

Approaches to Innovation

Adjacencies

The theory of Adjacencies developed by George Day and Roch Parayre of the Wharton School of Business is one of the easiest models to use to think about innovation. Any enterprise can be improved by using this model. One of the other great advantages to this approach is that it limits risk by only focusing your change initiative on one aspect of the operation at a time.

You always start an adjacencies innovation by thinking about your current product or service and your current customer. Think about this carefully, because you might have people using your facility who are not paying. Whether or not you are currently getting money from them, they are your customers and they are people who have a relationship with your organization. Also, think carefully about your product or service. Here again, people may be appreciating something about your offerings that you are not recognizing as a product or service.

An example of a product or service that you are not thinking about as such could be a special place in a park where people come to see some kind of birds. In that scenario, you have a unique product and a group of customers you may not be focused on because they do not consume your staff resources, but it is a product and they are customers all the same. And they have a certain loyalty or affinity to your organization. Using this example, maybe you start offering bird identification books for sale at your facility or offering a class in bird identification and advertise it with post-ers in the parking lot the birders use. You have a unique market that you can expand on if you understand it as such. The key is to put yourself in the minds of your customers and think about their experiences, then think about who else might like such an experience and determine how to reach them.

With the adjacencies model in Figure 5.1, think about a current cus-tomer and a current product or service. Then take one step outward on either the horizontal or vertical axis. By changing or expanding just one variable customer or product/service, you are reducing your risk. There is sometimes a temptation to go into an entirely unknown enterprise, one in which you do not have an existing relationship with the customer base and do not have in-depth experience with the product/service. This type

In a rapidly changing world,

we must ALL be innovators to succeed.

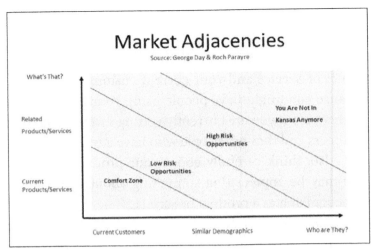

Figure 5.1. Adjacency Model

of enterprise is extremely risky. Moving one step on just one of the axes is a very controlled risk. You either know the customer and are just offering a new product/service, or you have expertise with the product/service and are just looking for an expanded customer base.

Using the adjacency model, let's examine the business or market of offering picnic shelter rentals. Groups of 50 to 200 people are renting these shelters for the day to have family gatherings, corporate outings, church or club gatherings, etc. You could just rent the pavilion and leave it at that, or you could think about who your users are and what would make their experiences better and start innovation along the adjacency axis.

Using your current customers and moving just one step up the product/service axis, you could start offering food catering, moon bounces and other games that a large group might like. This is the best direction to start, because finding customers is the most challenging task in most enterprises. It is much easier to up-sell a current customer than it is to find a new customer. The food and games are things that many of your shelter renters will need or want for their event. By offering these services as a one-stop shop, you have just made the life of your customer that much easier. They no longer need to make five more phone calls or search the web for a company that can bring in the services they want for a great event. When you are thinking about expanding the product/service, do not think you need to do everything yourself. You can outsource the additional product/services with a partnership agreement, or you can do them internally if you have the expertise. Generally, partnering is a great way to start a new venture in a way that minimizes your risk. You can always decide to provide the service/product internally later, once you know the business better and if you think there is an advantage to doing so.

Moving one step to the right is taking your existing product/service and looking for new customers. While this can be challenging, it is an important process to go through. You already have a winning offering, but only a small segment of the potential market knows about it. How do you identify similar groups/customers to the ones you already have that might be interested? The more targeted you can get in your marketing efforts, the more successful you will be. In the model below, corporate groups are the new market that is being explored. You might go through the Chamber of Commerce to identify companies in your community over a certain size and then target their human resources departments with information about great full-service corporate gatherings. Find a similar group that has used your pavilions and get a glowing testimonial about the wonderful day they had at your facility and how it built their team and made them more productive.

While the two examples of expanding a service to an existing customer or expanding the customers for an existing service are both very sound

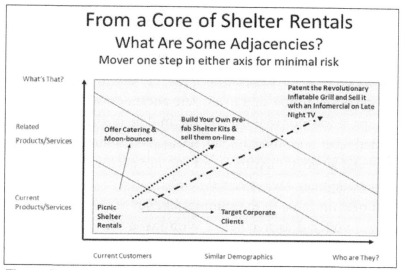

Figure 5.2. One Step Along Axis to Reduce Risk

business approaches with a high chance of success and a low level of risk, the other two examples on the model in Figure 5.2 get farther and farther afield of a sound business model for an organization that is in the business of renting picnic shelters.

As a child, whenever my family would visit a popular or scenic destination, my father would always say that it was the perfect place to open a family pie shop. He actually did not make pies, never worked in any food service operation, and did not know anything about the area beyond that of a tourist passing through. But opening a pie shop right there seemed like a great business venture. Now, I know that many of these announcements of a new pie shop venture were designed to get a reaction from my mother, and they always did. However, it is an example of the impulse to take a business risk without enough knowledge of the product/service or the customer/market. The adjacency model of innovation is a great way to keep driving continued innovation and improvements in your operations, without taking the "pie shop risk" of entering a venture you do not really know in a market that you are not connected with. Many people make the mistake of thinking that every business or enterprise that seems busy from a customer perspective must be a great enterprise to get into. In reality, some of the best enterprises to get into are the ones you do not see on every corner, because they have not already been exploited by the competition. This is where innovation comes in.

Below is an actual adjacency innovation from Great Waves Waterpark in Alexandria, Virginia. For years, the waterpark, which features a large wave pool as the central attraction rented inflatable tubs to ride the waves. The tube shack had an attendant who was very busy in the morning when people checked out a tube, and in the late afternoon when they returned it, but the space was not well used in the middle of the day. Since some people rented tubes and some did not, it was also a source of conflict when someone would let go of their tube and another person would take it, perhaps not knowing that it was a rental item.

The innovation came in the summer of 2009 when, for the first time, the tubes were offered as free items. With just a stack of tubes on deck, there was no need to tie up a building and attendant to dispense the tubes. A small per-person price increase for the whole waterpark made up the amount the tube rentals used to bring in. Then the building in its central location was transformed into the "shark shack," a creatively decorated building that made people want to see what it was all about (Figures 5.3 and 5.4). The former tube attendant was now busy all day selling retail items to the thousands of waterpark customers who would typically spend 5 to 7 hours at the waterpark. The area in front of the shark shack was stocked with retail items such as sunscreen, hats, towels, beads, sunglasses, and more. In years two and three, with more experience, the inventory of products was tweaked to stock items that were more popular, and sales continued to rise.

Figure 5.3. Using Adjacency Theory To Add Retail Operations

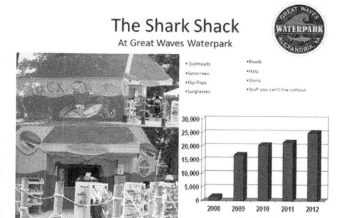

Figure 5.4. Shark Shack Retail

This was an adjacency innovation where we took the current customer base and offered an added product/service that enhanced the customer experience.

What operation would not like to have additional $20,000 + in revenue and $10,000 to $15,000 in additional net income without additional staffing expense and no real capital improvements? These kinds of innovation can and should be a regular diet for agencies that use the adjacency model to think about all of their current operations.

Blue Ocean Strategy

Blue Ocean Strategy is a book discussing the theory developed by Chan Kim and Renee Mauborgne (2005), and is the most exciting model in innovation thinking. The name comes from the idea that when you are offering products/services that are similar to your competitors, you are fighting for market share in direct competition, and the ocean is red with the blood from fighting. Some organizations are able to create products/services so unique that the competition becomes irrelevant. Those great innovators create market spaces that they own, and those are true Blue Ocean innovations.

The book by Kim and Mauborgne highlights a number of great examples of organizations that have created new markets. Cirque du Soleil started with the appealing element of going to the theater, cut out the number one expense of traditional circuses, which was the animals, and came up with a new formula and product. Starbucks created a market for coffee bars that did not exist on a wide scale before they introduced the American market to high-quality coffee served in an upscale environment. And Yellow Tail Wine created a new market for wine that was easy for consumers who were not familiar with wine to understand and appreciate.

One of the tools of Blue Ocean Strategy is the "Strategic Canvas," where you rank a product against the competition (Figure 5.5). Most people start with the perception that you need to meet or exceed the competition at every level to win. This strategy leads to high cost and low price, which is

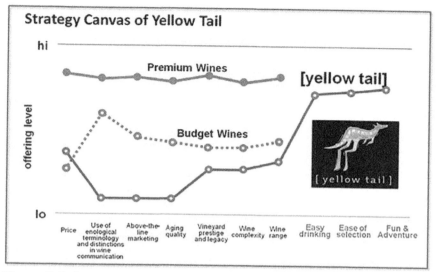

Figure 5.5. Strategic Canvas

not a strategy for success. Blue Ocean Strategy is about adding value that the competition does not offer. These may be values the consumers are not yet aware of, since they are not currently available. At the same time, decide what are the cost drivers that you will not want to compete on. In this way, you create a product/service that has unique values to the customer, and a lower cost of delivery.

Notice in the Yellow Tail Wine Strategic Canvas that both the high end and budget wines were competing in a similar way, and no one was offering easy to select and fun wines. The rest were all trying to play in the fancy wine market, not realizing that there was a huge untapped market of beer drinkers who might switch to wine if it were made easy.

Yellow Tail produced an inexpensive wine and made it easy and fun to drink by making it obvious on the label what kind of food to match with the wine and painting a picture of the good times the wine would deliver (Figure 5.6).

Just like with adjacencies, the innovation comes from thinking about the customer's experience. But with Blue Ocean, the innovation creates a new and uncontested market space.

Figure 5.6. Yellow Tail Win

An example of Blue Ocean Strategy in the parks, recreation, and tourism field can be seen at the waterparks run by the Northern Virginia Regional Park Authority (NVRPA). In 2008, NVRPA had two successful waterparks and three that were struggling. Two of those three were losing money on their operations, and the other was about break even. There was a perception from decades of running pools and waterparks that theming was a frivolous expense, and the way to enhance a waterpark was to buy a big slide or other feature from the various vendors of those kinds of items. This strategy had worked in the past but was very expensive. This was a red ocean strategy of playing the same game as all the competition did.

With both the need to enhance the performance of the worst of the pools, and lacking the funds and time it would take to install many major new features, a Blue Ocean Strategy was born. And it was called "Pirate's Cove Waterpark" (Figure 5.7).

Rather than trying to build a generic waterpark with many expensive features, NVRPA thought about the customer. They realized that the most influential decision maker about where the family goes for their waterpark experience is the 4- to 10-year-old child in the family. Of course parents, particularly mothers in most cases, are the final deciders on where the family will go for their waterpark fun, but they are significantly influenced

Pirate's Cove Waterpark

Creating a Destination

Before

After

Figure 5.7. Pirate's Cove Waterpark

by the 4- to 10-year-olds in the family. If these children are sold on a destination, they will influence where the whole family goes. This is an age of imagination, and exciting that imagination is more important than any large feature you could add.

So, a pirate theme was selected. From the first books about pirates that came out in the 1680s, to the most recent movies about them, pirates have captured the imagination of the public and always excited a sense of adventure (Figure 5.8). A pirate-themed feature was put in the center of the shallow end of the pool, with a dumping bucket and small slides and water cannons. More importantly, the whole facility was themed. The entire pool building looked like a ship, with a tall mast and furrowed sail, cannon ports bristled on the side of the building with lapping waves painted along the length of the building. The grassy circle in front of the building, where people can drive up, was transformed into a sandy island with palm trees in the center. By starting the theming on the outside, the unique experience of the waterpark started the minute it came into view, and the excitement of what it had to offer began there. Inside the lobby, realistic-looking fiberglass pirates climbed on ropes above the heads of patrons. A sand play area was created that was seeded with gold treasure. When children found the treasure, they could redeem it for a pirate-themed prize.

To market the new feature, an annual Pirate Day was established at the beginning of summer where pirate re-enactors came in for a weekend and fought mock battles, taught the children how to sing sea shanties, pull ropes, fight with swords, and other essential pirate skills. The event yielded good press for the park, and the popularity climbed (Figure 5.9).

Figure 5.8. Adding a Sense of Adventure to Aquatics

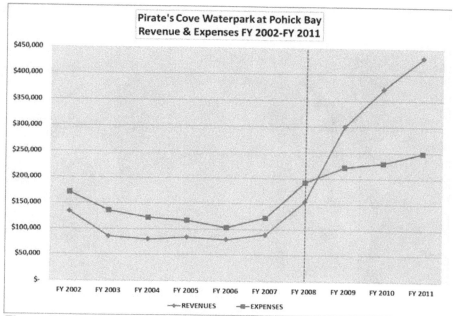

Figure 5.9. 2008 Theming and Renovation

While a large slide tower (also pirate-themed) was added in 2012, the success of Pirate's Cove Waterpark came from offering the public a unique experience that no other waterpark in the region could provide. It recognized that children were the most important customers for this type of facility and engaged their imaginations. On the following page you can see the impact of this 2008 renovation/innovation.

In 2009, the success of the Blue Ocean Strategy of creating a compelling theme that engaged the imagination of children was used again, as another underperforming pool was remade into Atlantis (Figure 5.10). The ancient Greek-themed waterpark featured mermaids and Poseidon and looked like an ancient Greek temple. Again, it created a unique experience unlike anything else offered, and again, that unique experience was key to enhanced performance (Figure 5.11).

2010 brought a similar transformation with the creation of Volcano Island Waterpark, complete with the best volcano in the region, giant Easter Island stone heads on the deck (Figure 5.12) , lots of thatch and lots of palm trees.

Figure 5.10. Atlantis

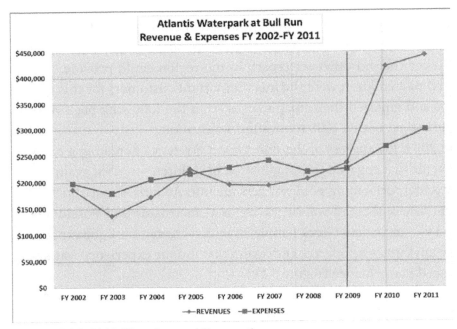

Figure 5.11. 2009 Theming and Renovation

Figure 5.12. Polynesia Theming at Volcano Island Water

With each of these projects, while some new waterpark features were added, the focus was on creating a unique and compelling experience the user would have. By making a unique experience, the competition became irrelevant. NVRPA was not selling thousands of gallons of chlorinated water with a concrete deck, slides, and food concessions, it was selling adventure and imagination.

Another way to think about a Blue Ocean Strategy is to think of the "value innovation" (Figure 5.13). How do you lower your cost and at the same time offer customers a unique value? In the case of the NVRPA waterparks, the cost savings were needed to invest less in traditional waterpark features and to create value through the compelling theming.

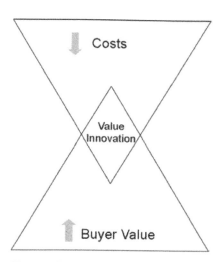

Figure 5.13. Value Innovation key to Blue Ocean Strategy

Disruptive Innovation

The theory of Disruptive Innovation (Figure 5.14) was developed by Clayton Christensen of Harvard Business School (1997). Christensen's theory focuses primarily on technology. He looked at how innovators in technology often wind up making products that surpass the needs of the average consumer. When this happens, it opens an opportunity for another company to come along with a product that does not offer all the bells and whistles of the tech leader but meets most of the needs of the average users and does so at a lower price point. When this happens, the newer product in the market can capture a large market share.

An example of how a disruptive innovation has affected the parks, recreation,and tourism economy could be seen with the Nintendo Wii game. On Wii you can play tennis, bowl, fence, golf, play baseball and other games. The cost of playing Wii is significantly less than the cost of playing any one of these sports. While for some who really love these games, Wii is a poor substitute, for others, the Wii may be all the bowling (or other sport) they ever need, and they will not contribute/participate in the "real" version of the sport with its high cost.

If you can be the organization that can come up with the lower cost, easier to use alternative that achieves all that many people want from a field, you can have a very successful business model.

Disruptive Innovations

Old Market Dominance	New Market Dominance
• Department Stores ⟶	• Discount Retailers
• Tax Preparers ⟶	• Turbo Tax
• Large Mainframe computers ⟶	• Personal Computers
• Desktop computer ⟶	• Smartphone
• Encyclopedias ⟶	• Wikipedia/Google
• Pay Phones ⟶	• Cell Phones
• Travel Agents ⟶	• Travelocity/Orbitz

Figure 5.14. Disruptive Innovations

The recreation field is in need of more significant innovation. Many parks and recreation facilities around the country look and operate nearly identical to the way they did years ago, and are nearly identical to count-less others like them across the nation. From a technology perspective, the big invention over the last decade has been the artificial turf field, allowing much greater play per field than ever before. While this has been a good step forward, to be relevant in a changing world, the parks, recreation and tourism field needs to change and innovate at a much faster pace.

With the great explosion of mobile applications being developed, and the tremendous growth in the use of smartphones forecast for the coming years, new applications may be a hotbed of disruptive innovation in the years ahead.

Pricing

Understand Cost Recovery and Market Pricing

Pricing is a combination of accounting, market awareness, and philosophy. The philosophical part of pricing comes into play more in the public sector, where "public" tax dollars are going to subsidize some elements of the agency. Some of that subsidy comes from the capital funds that went into building the facilities and acquiring the land. In most public agencies, virtually all of the capital (with the exception of grants and gifts) has been funded through tax dollars. An exception would be land or facilities built with revenue bonds that need to be paid back to the lender with funds generated from those facilities. On the operating side, it is most likely more of a mix with some of the operating costs of the agency being funded with tax dollars and some through user fees (enterprise operations). Wherever there are public dollars invested, there should be "public benefit" in the form of some value that is being provided to the broader community.

Good pricing can do more than recover costs,

it can create VALUE.

Some programs and facilities are not intended to recover their costs in a direct fashion because they serve different public needs. A midnight basketball program in an otherwise high crime part of a city might reduce crime and give youth healthy alternatives. Those outcomes are of high public value, so you do not need or want to charge for that service. A museum that attracts tourists to your community who stay in hotels and eat at local restaurants may be an operation that a community will want to subsidize with tax dollars because it generates tax income for them.

Some agencies with ample tax dollar funding might not choose to focus on cost recovery, and that is okay if the community has decided that all or most programs and activities should be free or heavily subsidized. For other agencies, it is less of a choice and more of a necessity to earn adequate revenue to support and grow the organization and its mission.

One of the unique and wonderful things about public sector parks and recreation agencies is that unlike most other elements of government, they have a choice and can earn more funds than are provided from tax dollars. This is very empowering, and embracing this option is a central part of the entrepreneurial approach. While there is often a desire to offer the public services at deeply discounted rates (or for free), it is also important to realize that a public park agency may be in competition with the private sector for services. There is nothing wrong with this competition if the products/ services are being priced to cover full costs, but if they are subsidized, it creates an unfair market for the private sector.

Creating Value

Free products or services are often not valued. What this means is that people put a higher value or importance on items that have a cost. And sometimes the higher the cost, the more that item is seen as important.

Creating value is an interesting process, because it involves both the consumer and the product or service provider. In the end, the value is what the customer thinks is a fair price, which might be significantly higher or lower than the cost. So, while cost and cost recovery are important, it is something different and ultimately less important than the customer's perceived value.

Perceived value is driven by customer expectation more than anything else. If you have a golf course, the perceived value can have a lot to do with other courses in the area. Are you next to a high-end private course or a cheap, run-down par 3 course? In one case, the golfing community might think that anything under $100 for 18 holes is a great deal, and in another they might think that anything over $25 is a bad deal. This is

an issue of "framing." What is the customer expecting to pay based on similar products they are aware of?

One of the factors that will create more or less value is the message you are sending your customers with your pricing strategy. Ideally, what you want to do with the customer is to build a relationship that will foster customer loyalty and repeat business. What often happens is that there is a perception that the relationship is one sided and focused on extracting maximum money from them for providing the experience or product. Balancing the goal of building a relationship with that of a profitable transaction is important.

Amazon Prime

A good model of a relationship-building pricing policy is that of Amazon Prime. In 2005, Amazon rolled out this new program that would give customers free and faster shipping on many items for $99 per year. This service addressed the one downside of online purchasing, which is ship-  ping costs and delays, and at the same time gave an incentive to prime members to buy even more from Amazon and maximize the value of this fixed-price deal.

Framing Expectations
*What are the Known Values that Your
Product/Service are Connected to?*

Sell the Encyclopedia, and the Computer is Free

In the early days of home computers, most people did not have a good sense of what a computer was worth, since for many if was the first time they were buying one for personal use.

Bill Gates understood this challenge, and he solved it by acquiring the rights to an encyclopedia. He renamed this data base "Encarta" and gave a free CD with this encyclopedia included with every new computer that was running a Microsoft operating system.

For years, encyclopedias had been sold as large collections of beautiful hardbound books. A set of these would cost around $2,000. Everyone knew that a good set of encyclopedias would set you back by that amount, and everyone knew that having an encyclopedia set in your home was a good thing and would help your children with school projects.

So the sales pitch in those days was that if you bought the computer, which cost around $2,000, you were essentially buying an encyclopedia (which you knew was of high value) and getting the computer, which was more of a gamble, for free.

It did not matter that the CD with the Encarta encyclopedia had a cost of less than $.15, the computer was now framed as having a value of at least $2,000, and, as a result, millions were sold.

The key that made this pricing strategy successful was that it showed an understanding of what their best customers were worried about, and it built a long-term and repeat business relationship with those who preferred online shopping.

Golf Memberships

Just like Amazon Prime addressed the needs of the regular online shopper, the same has been done by numerous park agencies that have introduced golf membership programs for their golf courses. These programs offer unlimited play for those who pay an annual fixed cost membership fee. Some memberships are for weekday-only play, some might be unlimited or offer a discount rate for seniors, but they all offer an unlimited number of plays for a fixed annual rate. The advantage to the regular player is a reduced rate. The advantage to the park agency that owns the golf course is that it gets money up front, regardless of weather. This kind of program also locks those regular golfers into the agency's courses vs. those golfers playing many courses over the year. If the agency divides the membership revenue over 12 months and recognizes that revenue evenly over the year, it means that even in the worst weather conditions the course will be recognizing its membership revenue.

If such programs are focused on low usage times like weekdays, they can be extremely effective. A golf course is largely a fixed cost operation. It costs a little over a million dollars a year to run one, whether you have five rounds of golf or 50,000 rounds played in a year. Because the costs are fixed and not variable, there is very little additional cost per player, and the goal is to drive a total gross revenue that is greater than the annual fixed costs.

These programs build course loyalty, whereas a one-time discount does not. Where such programs do not work is if the price is set way too low or the discounted members take up all the prime tee times that others would pay a lot more for. Both of those factors can be managed in a successful program, and the result can be year-round revenue, an insurance policy against poor weather, and customer loyalty among the 5% to 10% of players who want to play often.

Cost Recovery Models

Many public parks and recreation agencies have some kind of cost-recovery policy or model. Even where there is not a formal adopted policy, an informal model usually exists. The benefit of having an adopted policy of this type is that it helps the agency deal with the constant push for free or subsidized services in a fair manner.

The basic elements of most cost-recovery policies is that they make a clear difference between produces/services that benefit a broad cross section of the community and meet the goals of the government and those that benefit a small group or an individual.

So, if access to public open space and nature is important to the community, the park should not have an entrance fee. However, if there are food concessions or a merry-go-round in the park, those things only benefit the individual and should be priced to recover 100% of the cost of operation or more.

If a community decides that it wants to subsidize youth sports for the societal benefits it provides, such as reducing childhood obesity and keeping youth from getting involved in drugs and crime, then it can subsidize these costs with tax dollars. The same community might decide that while the benefits of youth sports are great, it will not subsidize adult sports because it does not provide that same community benefit; rather, it is more of an individual (or small group) benefit. Under this scenario, the policy might price adult sports at a premium above its expense so the net funds can be used to subsidize youth sports. Whatever the priorities are, a policy allows for the pricing decisions to be transparent and consistent. Without such a policy, the agency is too apt to be blown in the political winds. The time to decide what to charge for athletic programs is not when the mayor has been approached by an adult or youth sports league about a "deal." Develop your policy ahead of time, so that you are approaching cost recovery from a consent and fair perspective.

An example of cost recovery without consideration to a model of differentiation between community vs. individual benefits can be seen in the reaction of a number of state park systems in the wake of the Great Recession. Many faced with deep budget problems considered putting in place a standard per-person or per-car charge to enter all of their parks. Fortunately, most of the systems thought twice and came up with a more differentiated model. Charging everyone a standard cost to access public lands creates an obstacle for the public to access the lands they bought with their tax dollars. In an ideal model, access to natural spaces should be free, and

Selling More by Taking Less
An Example of Changing the Value Proposition

The Northern Virginia Regional Park Authority sells annual launch passes for kayaks and canoes that are called "car-top launch passes" since the users generally carry their boats on car-top roof racks.

For a number of years, this item generated $4,000 to $6,000 annually for the agency. In 2007, NVRPA set up a paddling group called the Occoquan Watertrail League (OWL). This group helped promote the use of the water trail, safety on the water, and environmental stewardship.

In setting up the group, NVRPA agreed to set aside 20% of the car-top launch sales into an account that OWL could use for stewardship and club activities. At the time, there was some discussion within NVRPA that we were giving up needed revenue. The other side of the discussion was that by creating a club, they would both gain volunteers as well as attract more people to buy the annual pass, resulting in more money over time.

It was a gamble, but one with a sound theory behind it. The result was that the club sales of the annual pass shot up, so by 2012 NVRPA was selling not $6,000 as it had in 2007, but over $17,000 in car-top launch passes.

"A rising tide lifts all boats," and rising sales meant that NVRPA had improved revenues and had created a great ally and source of volunteers in the new Occoquan Watertrail League.

value-added extra services should be attractive and priced in such a way that they offer a good value and cover the costs of the park operations.

A robust cost-recovery model takes value-added programs and services, and it is not something that is easy to implement overnight. It needs to be a core part of the agency's philosophy, so it is something that is thought about over time, so investments can be made in attractive facilities and programs that are priced from the beginning in a manner that covers all the costs and generates extra funds that can help offset other costs.

One of the great things about focusing on a successful cost-recovery model is that it is much more than just charging fees. The fee only works if the product or service is seen as valuable to the customer. And the focus on the customer experience means that high-value parks, recreation, and tourism facilities and programs will be offered. If the model is fully or largely subsidized, then there is much less focus on the customers because they are not critical to success. Subsidized programs can see waning usage for years and be kept around because of inertia such as, "We have always done it that way." In a revenue-focused agency/facility, there is a need for constant improvement and staying attuned to the market and customer. In this way, the public can sometimes be better served by revenue programs than subsidized ones.

Cost-Based Pricing

Central to the revenue recovery model is to understand costs and charge an appropriate price to recover 100% or more of those costs. This approach requires an understanding of two categories of costs: direct and indirect.

Related to the terms direct and indirect (defined below) are two other terms:

Fixed costs = Those costs that are there regardless of how many units of your product/service are sold. This is often looked at as "overhead" or the costs associated with running the organization.

Variable costs = Those costs that are directly connected to offering the product like the costs of consumable materials.

Labor cost can be either fixed or variable. Full-time staff needed to run the organization like accounting, law enforcement, management, and so forth, are all fixed costs. A seasonal employee brought in for just peak times to offer a product/service, such as a yoga instructor just hired for the hours that the yoga class is being conducted, would be part of the variable cost of offering that service.

Direct costs. This category includes all the direct materials and labor costs needed to supply a given service or program. Many times prices are chosen without in-depth consideration of what the direct costs are. Without this understanding, it is very possible to generate revenue and loss at the same time. As the old saying goes, "We might lose money on every deal, but we make it up in volume."

But understanding direct costs is just the first step. It is also essential to have an estimate of the total volume, or units sold, that you will have, and the market price for similar products/services. To come up with a cost per unit, you need to divide your direct costs by the expected units sold. This gives you a basement price. Anything less than this will create a loss. Setting the price on just the direct costs is called "marginal cost pricing." Such an approach looks primarily (or solely) at variable costs.

Understanding the market price for the product/service is equally essential. If your competitive prices are below your direct costs, your costs are out of line. Ideally, you can create unique products/services that do not have direct competition. Then you can establish the going rate for the service/product that provides full cost recovery.

In-direct costs. Indirect costs include organizational expenses such as maintenance, insurance, marketing, capital costs for the facilities, and overhead costs of your headquarters, including accounting, legal, and management, and so forth.

"Full cost accounting" includes all of the direct and in-direct costs. Optimally, all of these costs should be included if the goal is to move toward 100% cost recovery. A great place to find the data on full costs is the Comprehensive Annual Financial Report (CAFR), more commonly known as the "Audit." One of the newer financial reporting standards that public sector agencies need to comply with now requires full cost accounting that breaks each facility or area of operations down with its full costs, including capital facilities. Full cost accounting factors in both variable and fixed costs.

Price-Based Costing

So, now we know how to add up all of our costs, estimate the number of units we will sell, and divide the costs by the units to come up with full-cost pricing. The problem with this method is that it assumes the costs are not controllable. Such an approach can often lead to prices that are too high and a general lack of efficiency. It also assumes your customers will buy the product/service at that price.

Most people don't fully consider that for any issue there are multiple possible solutions. Instead, it is tempting to settle on the first solution and assume that is it. So, as you start to offer a product or service, you buy a bunch of stuff (materials), hire a bunch of people and make your product or service. If you just focus on cost-based pricing, you might never consider that many other approaches to delivering the product/service are out there. And, you might never consider how to enhance your efficiency.

Price-Based Costing
An Example of a Radical Model for Creating a Product for a Target Market

Tata Motors, a large automotive manufacturer in India, realized that even the most inexpensive cars on the market were too expensive for many in India who own small motorcycles for their family transportation. If they could make a car for about $1,800, they would tap a huge new market. So they designed a car that could be made and sold for that price point, and the result was the Nano.

It uses a motorcycle engine, no rear hatch, only one rear mirror and only 3 nuts per wheel. But it is a car, and it sells for less than $2,000, and there is a huge demand for it.

It is only possible because they designed the car to meet a desired price point instead of adding up expenses for things that seemed essential.

Price-based costing is a process of starting with the end product. You are selling something to the customer. What price would the customer like to pay? What price would put you where you would like to be in the market?

Now take that price, multiply it by how many units you think you will sell at that price point, and that will give you your total. Now back out of it the amount you think should go to fixed costs and profit margin, and then you have what is available to cover direct costs. It will be less than you had hoped for. Bring together a team and start coming up with approaches that live within the available funds. This will not be the first approach of "buy a bunch of stuff and hire a bunch of people." You will need to think creatively and consider numerous scenarios. In the process, you will become very aware of the key cost drivers in whatever venture you are considering. As you consider what costs to cut, it will bring you around to thinking about what it is exactly that most customers value about this product/service. If you can cut the expenses that only a small segment of your customers value and offer a product that offers high value in the areas that are most important, and do so at a lower cost, you have a winner.

While it was business guru Peter Drucker who introduced the idea of price-based costing, if you can do so effectively and offer the core value that most (not all) of the customers are looking for at a lower price point, you have just created a "Disruptive Innovation" in the language of Harvard Business School Professor Clayton Christensen. The biggest challenge in this approach is that it requires you to challenge conventional thinking, to break away from the "this is the way we do it" approach that is in every organization to one degree or another.

While full-cost pricing is an important model to understand, the most important lesson in pricing is that there is almost no relationship between costs and the perceived value that the customer places on your product/service. So the key goal is to understand the customer and how he or she views your offerings enough to create value.

Marketing

How to Be Proactive in the Sales of Your Offerings

At the 1976 NRPA Congress, Dr. John L. Crompton was asked to present at a national conference on park marketing...and only a handful of people showed up for his session. "It was totally embarrassing. Nobody at that time realized marketing, which is something business-related, had anything to do with parks and recreation," reflected Dr. Crompton about that day. This story reveals a change that has occurred in the field over the last 30+ years. Parks, recreation, and tourism have transitioned from a pure government service supported by tax dollars and rather uniform in its offering, into a much more dynamic field that is part of the local/regional economy, can be increasingly self-supported financially, and offering an ever wider number of unique services to meet changing customer desires.

The question is, has the approach to marketing changed for parks and recreation agencies over the decades? Traditionally, most public sector agencies have had a Public Information Officer model of external communications. This model is one where media releases are put out that cover the who, what, when, and where of events, and there is a hope that news outlets will pick up this "news" and cover these events. The same basic information is put on the agency's website and community calendars. This makes the information accessible if someone is looking for it. This mode of communication is called "pull" because it requires the public to seek the information out. It is also presented in a dispassionate, just-the-facts manner.

Marketing is all about proactively driving the actions of a potential customer. The "pull" mode of communication does not drive any action, it just makes information available if someone is seeking it out (Figure 7.1). This no-pressure, just-the-facts mode is okay for other government agencies that are not trying to compete for the public's time and money, but it is completely out of date for the entrepreneurial park, recreation, or tourism organization of today.

Another significant factor that has changed the environment for getting your message out is the death of local newspapers. A decade ago, there were local papers in most communities that would cover the just-the-facts news releases that the public information officers would put out. That made the old model work to some degree. Over the last decade, local newspapers have been in a death spiral with most already out of business or fast heading that way. Without the friendly local newspaper with reporters covering anything put out, a much more targeted approach is essential for success.

Is Your Model Passive or Active?

pull
PIO Model
Public Information Officer

- Put out news releases about the: who, what, when and where of programs.
- The public will seek out the programs and facilities they are interested in.

push
Marketing Model
Proactive Marketing

- You are competing for limited leisure time/money.
- You understand who you are selling to, and what they want.
- Marketing effort are designed to drive actions.

Figure 7.1. PIO vs. Marketing Model

If you are willing to offer a product or service,

you have to be willing to aggressively market it.

The "push" model of communication is the marketing model. In this model, you are proactively seeking out your potential customers, selling them on your product/service, and attempting to drive the purchasing action. For many in the public sector, this may feel too high pressure. However, it is essential for success. If nothing else, we are competing for people's leisure time.

Recent studies from the National Golf Foundation have found that time is now a bigger obstacle than money and is keeping people from playing more golf. This same dynamic is most likely true for most other recreational activities.

Most people have many more potential options for how to spend their leisure time than they did a generation ago. Unlimited TV options with a huge number of channels plus services like Netflix, Hulu, and YouTube, and an explosion of web- and mobile-based entertainment options, Wii and XBox, all lead to less time spent in outdoor recreation. The sooner our field embraces that we are in competition for customers the better we will be. The average person today is exposed to a huge number of marketing messages. If parks, recreation, and tourism rely on the communication methods of a different generation, it will not succeed.

Sally Jewell, former CEO of REI (current U.S. Secretary of the Interior) was talking with the CEO of Best Buy and was asked who her main competitor was. She answered "Best Buy." This answer was very insightful. It is not that Ms. Jewell did not realize that other companies sell backpacks,

Sally Jewel

kayaks, bikes, and boats. It is that she realizes that the larger competitor for outdoor recreation is all the other things people can now do without leaving home. This is why competing for that limited leisure time is more important now than ever before.

Gaining Exposure
Example of Social Media Marketing

Tom Starnes
Communications Manager, Orange County Parks, CA

In January 2011, a wild bald eagle appeared at Irvine Regional Park and began vocalizing with a female bald eagle, "Olivia," at the park's OC Zoo. Wild bald eagles are very rare in this mostly urban environment, so a zookeeper shot video of the visiting eagle and posted it on the OC Parks YouTube channel, as well as stills on its Flickr account. Staff posted links to the video from OC Parks Facebook and Twitter accounts, which got multiple "likes," comments, and retweets, including by the local newspaper's Twitter account. OC Parks PIO contacted the local newspaper, the *Orange County Register*, and pitched the story, referring the reporter to the YouTube video. The timeliness—just two weeks before Valentine's Day—helped give the story a love angle. The reporter ran the story and link to the video on the *Register*'s website. Staff posted links to the story on our Facebook and Twitter and continued generating comments, views, and attention. The *Los Angeles Times*, which rarely covers Orange County, got stunning photos of the visiting eagle and ran a story on the front page of its Sunday California section. The next day,

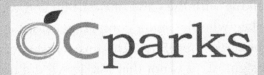

three Los Angeles television news outlets covered the story, and it got mentions on multiple morning radio shows. OC Parks held a "Name the Eagle" contest on its Facebook page. The OC Parks Commission picked the winning name. The winners received an annual parks pass and a behind-the-scenes tour of the zoo.

Different types of media that covered this story were major print media, local print media, local television news, radio mentions, national and local news websites, blogs, Facebook, and Twitter. The story received nearly full-page placement, above the fold, on the front pages of the local sections of the *Orange County Register* and the Sunday *Los Angeles Times*. KABC-TV and KCBS-TV came to the zoo to film news packages that aired and KNBC-TV also covered the story on its website. The Discovery Channel's website, among other national sites, featured the story, as did numerous blogs. A recent Google search turned up 419,000 hits for OC Zoo Eagle. OC Parks' YouTube channel doubled its views in one month. The eagle video received 18,000 views in two weeks and 19,400 as of this writing.

OC Parks tracks its media coverage using Cision, an industry leader in this field. Media coverage of this story led to the largest single month since OC Parks began monitoring media coverage this way, totaling 290 million total broadcast, print, Internet, and social media impressions. Cision estimated the dollar value of this coverage to be more than half a million dollars. This is compared to 39 million impressions and $33,000 for all media coverage the previous January—typically a slow month for the parks.

This coverage resulted in increased recognition and awareness for the OC Zoo. The small zoo features animals of the southwestern United States—the very animals that park visitors may encounter in OC Parks' wilderness parks. While the zoo is in one of OC Parks' most popular facilities, Irvine Regional Park, it is often considered a "hidden gem" that many people have yet to hear about. OC Parks has been working hard over the past two years to raise the profile of zoo. The publicity generated by the eagle media coverage resulted in increased awareness of the OC Zoo, and its visitation increased by 40% over the same month the previous year. The ocparks.com website received a 31% increase in visits during the two-week height of publicity, compared to the same time period the previous year; the zoo's page on the website saw a 142% increase in visits. The OC Parks

Facebook page saw an 80% increase in post views to 70,000 in those two weeks and a 182% increase in post feedback (likes and comments). The name-the-eagle contest, OC Parks' first Facebook contest, had more than 600 views and 70 entries, far exceeding expectations. This resulted not only in positive external communications, but positive internal communications.

Understanding Your Customer

Any successful marketing effort is rooted in a good understanding of your customer. And understanding the customer has something to do with who they are from a demographic perspective (age, gender, income, etc.) but much more to do with their psychographic profile. Psychographic factors relate to values, attitudes, interests, or lifestyles and are much stronger indicators of behavior than demographics are (Figure 7.2).

Who are your Customers?
Demographics and Psychographics

Demographics	Psychographics
• Age	• Interests
• Race	• Hobbies
• Income	• Values
• Education	• Lifestyle
• Family Size	• attitudes
• Geography	• Motivations

Within a demographic group there are numerous psychographic sub-groups.

Figure 7.2. Demographics vs. Psychographics

Values, interests, and hobbies are much more important indicators of future behaviors

than purely demographic factors.

An example of different demographics but similar psychographics would be two people:

Suzie

Demographics: 25 years old, female, Asian, single, earns $40,000/year, lives in an urban apartment with several friends.

Bob

Demographics: 55 years old, male, Caucasian, married with 2 children, earns $100,000/year, lives in a single family home in the suburbs.

Common Psychographic Interests

Bob cycles and Suzie is a rock climber; they both like outdoor adventures, they both hope to stretch their physical skills and explore nature more, they both seek out organic foods and read about healthy living options, are concerned about protecting the environment, and would like to have more time in a natural environment.

While neither Suzie nor Bob have ever gone kayaking before, from a psychographic perspective they are both perfect candidates for the new naturalist-led kayak trip that your agency is offering. This new program offers to teach introductory kayaking skills, provides all the equipment needed, and teaches the participants about the ecosystem that they will be paddling through. Bob and Suzie are great potential customers because they are interested in the environment and will learn from the naturalist,  and because they like outdoor adventures, have never kayaked before and will value the opportunity to learn how to do this outdoor sport they have not tried before. They will also both enjoy meeting like-minded environmentalists as part of this group.

Just looking at demographic information, you would never put Suzie and Bob in the same group because their demographics are different, but their values and interests are very similar, making them both ideal customers for your naturalist-led kayak trip.

Target Your Efforts

The world used to be dominated by broadcast media, newspapers, television, and radio. These media outlets were expensive and largely untargeted. Today, newspapers are quickly going out of business, magazines are struggling, and TV and radio are more fractured than they used to be. At the same time, the traditional media has been in decline, and there has been a great growth in social media, including Facebook, Twitter, Reddit, LinkedIn, and blogs. The bad news for marketers is that it is more challenging than ever before to figure out how best to reach your target audience. The good news is that it is potentially easier to do a better job of targeting smaller groups, and it is potentially much less expensive than it was when we were in a broadcast world.

In targeting Suzie and Bob for our kayak trip, you might want to think about where people gather both physically and online who have an interest in the environment and outdoor adventure. You could have a booth at a local farmers' market if you decided that people interested in locally grown and organic food would have values that would be the same as those interested in a naturalist-led kayak trip. You could also advertise or otherwise create a buzz on blogs and social media sites that cater to people with similar interests. Posting a YouTube video of enthusiastic participants at a similar program could give people other ways to find and share the experience.

If your agency has captured e-mails or cell phone numbers from participants in different programs, these can be extremely valuable. If you have a similar program and can send a message to past participants of similar programs, you are delivering a very targeted message. Be careful not to send the wrong message to the wrong group. Most people do not mind getting a message that connects with their interests but are rightfully annoyed at being sold something randomly.

Sell the Sizzle Not the Steak

The old "pull" communication model of just telling the who, what, where and when questions is not effective because it does not drive action. All of those details are important only if the potential customer has already decided to act. And what drives them to act is the answer to the "why" question. What deeply rooted emotional value will you gain by participating in this activity or buying this product? This positive emotional value is the sizzle. And you need to be able to communicate why this product/service is important and worth their time (Figure 7.3).

Sell the *Sizzle*

To be effective you must move beyond the description and sell the <u>benefits</u>.

Answer the question: **What emotional benefit are people getting from this?**

I am a good dad, and am building memories for life.

I am reconnected with nature, and will be stress free.

I am going to look and feel great.

Figure 7.3. Sell the Sizzle

Having an effective marketing message is as important as the delivery strategy of how the message will reach the target audience. This is a step that is often overlooked. Many people go straight to the sale when thinking about what to market/advertise. And while price is one of the key factors that affects the buying decision, it is sometimes not the only factor or even the most important factor. The power of a sale is much higher if the service/product is the same or very similar to others offered in your community. In those cases you are only selling price. If your product/service is unique, then you have market differentiation. You are selling something that is special, and you do not need to compete just on price, but can offer other unique values to the customers that others are not. Sometimes, we do not think about and value these differences in products as much as we should.

Analyze Your Market Position (SWOT)

The next step in creating a successful marketing plan is to fully understand your position in the marketplace. Is your product differentiated from the competition or very similar? What are other factors that affect how your offering is seen by your potential customers?

One of the most effective ways to get this view of how you are positioned in your market is to do a SWOT analysis. This approach looks at your position in the market from the perspective of strengths, weaknesses, opportunities and threats. This process is best done as a team exercise, as different people will be tuned into different elements. To view these issues from a market perspective, you need to answer these questions from the perspective of your customer. How do they look at what you offer compared to whatever alternatives might exist?

While understanding weaknesses and threats is good to have a complete picture of how you fit into the marketplace, no team ever won a game by just playing defense. The key to success (in every element of life) is to understand your strengths and take full advantage of those strengths and opportunities.

If you can use this process to then build a strategy that builds on the strengths of the organization and takes advantage of the opportunities, you will have a plan to move forward. In looking at the threats and weaknesses, ask your team if those deficiencies are significant enough that they are likely to derail your efforts. If the likelihood of this is low, put most of your effort behind the opportunities and strengths that can move the plan forward.

Marketing Plan

Whether your product or service is for a fee or free of charge, if it is important to bring people in, you should create a marketing plan. Such a plan can be done on many different scales and for many different budgets. A large agency might have a comprehensive marketing plan that covers everything from overall agency branding to different lines of business that exist. Such a plan will probably be connected to a marketing budget, and will include a combination of "earned media," which is free, and paid advertising. On the other end of the scale, you might create a marketing plan for one class or program at a single facility, and perhaps without a budget to support it. Large scale or small, planning is essential because it forces you to think about the issue in a systematic way. Dwight D. Eisenhower expressed this thought when he said "plans are useless, but planning is indispensable."

Low-Hanging Fruit

The best potential customer list you could have is the list of your current customers. They already have chosen your product/service once, and if they had a good experience, it will be easier to sell them again than it will to bring in an outside customer. You can approach selling your current customers in two ways:

1. Onsite marketing: signage and brochures at your facility
2. E-marketing to a database of current customers: using e-newsletter, and/or text messages

The first option is easy and inexpensive. Have signage that promotes products/services at that facility and other facilities that you operate. The entrance to your facility should have a brochure rack with information about other facilities in your system. As low tech as brochures are, they are still effective if properly placed in high traffic areas. In a recent parks and recreation needs assessment (survey), after word of mouth, brochures ranked as the second most common way the public learned of park offerings. This seems very out of date in the information technology world we live in today, but for a population with a wide range of age, income, and technology adoption, the simple brochure is still effective.

The second option requires you to have contact information about your customers. There are a number of ways to organically generate these lists (organically means self-generated vs. buying a list from a marketing firm). Here are a few options for generating such a data base:

- Simply offer an opportunity for people to sign up to get more information about your facility and future special offers.
- Offer an online discount that requires the participant to give you an e-mail and cell phone number to get the discount. This can be very effective.
- Offer a special onsite deal in which people scan a QR code with their smart phone; it will ask for their e-mail and cell phone number before displaying a coupon on their phone that can be redeemed for the offer (something like a free fountain drink).
- Offer cell phone interpretive messages so facility visitors can gain valuable information by calling a special number. In the process, you gain the information of their cell phone number that can be used for promotional text messages.

With this e-mail data you can customize an e-newsletter to address the issues that this customer segment is interested in. Such e-newsletters are very inexpensive and effective, but they should not be overused. An average of one message a month or every couple of weeks is about the limit without it becoming spam.

The cell phone data can be used for text marketing. These should be short messages with good offers. Again, they should not be overused, or they will be seen as spam. Much of the difference between spam and good information is the content. If your messages always have valuable content, they will be well received by most people.

A brochure rack, good facility signage, and e-mail newsletters to current customers should be a part of any marketing effort because they are all both effective and inexpensive. The other element of any marketing plan should be "earned media."

Viral Marketing
An Example of Tourism Marketing that
Used Creativity to Go Viral

Visit Fairfax, the destination marketing organization representing Fairfax County, Virginia, promoted tourism to the County by launching "Historical Figures," a creative campaign for smart phone users.

Fairfax County, Virginia
Connect with America

Transit posters, sandwich boards, and other displays in high traffic areas of New York, Philadelphia, and Washington, DC showed George Washington, Benjamin Franklin, and Thomas Jefferson with images of smart phones over their mouths. The public was encouraged to scan the QR code for each and hold their smart phone in front of the poster of the historic figure. This resulted in a video of the mouth of the founder pitching the attractions of visiting Fairfax County with numerous references to their own accomplishments. This creative application of technology and humor to sell the County that was home to George Washington was so successful that in the first six months over 150,000 people viewed this on Facebook, with over 16,000 watching the video on Facebook, over 2,600 people using the QR readers on their smart phones to experience the talking founders, and it generated over 400 media hits!

The ability to create a fun and interesting experience that people want to share through social media is the key to viral marketing. The great benefit of this approach is that it is not dependent on a giant marketing budget but rather on creativity to make it interesting enough so it will spread on its own.

Viral Marketing
Viewed by 150,000 people on Facebook

To cut through the barrage of marketing messages that everyone is exposed to each day, a higher premium needs to be placed on things like humor and creativity. And we need to create messages that focus less on the who, what, and where operational details of the product and more on the users' experience.

Financial Sustainability
Three Elements that All Park and Recreation Agencies Need to Succeed

Mary Beth Thaman
Director, Kettering, Ohio Parks and Recreation
Paul Gilbert
Executive Director, Northern Virginia Regional Park Authority

The field of parks and recreation is in transition. Many park and recreation systems are looking for ways to serve their communities in new ways, and with a funding mix that is more self-supporting than ever before. This can be the opening of new opportunities to provide value-added services to the community that help financially support the park and recreation facilities and programs that make a community stronger.

This model of greater self-sufficiency has been taught at the NRPA Revenue Development and Management School at Oglebay for 46 years. In 2012, the school experimented with a new session that generated great interest among the 90 participants. The new session was a facilitated discussion in small groups of the key role of the 3 Cs that are critical to success in the new world that we find ourselves in. The "3 Cs" coined by Regent Mary Beth Thaman, Director of Parks and Recreation for Kettering Ohio are as follows:

The Customer

The existence of parks and recreation services is determined by the demands of the customer. It is simple economics: supply and demand. The agency supply-

ing the programs and services that the customer demands at a price that generates revenue necessary to support the organization is going to succeed.

Basically, the more an agency can penetrate the market with the desirable programs and/or services demanded by the community, the more revenue and or community support will be generated. The key for an organization is collecting the correct data to understand the demands of the customer related to parks and recreation programs and services. This information will then drive the next C, core business.

The Core Business

Understanding the customer demands clearly will assist with prioritizing the core business of an agency. Parks and recreation agencies have notoriously created business models that attempt to provide all things to all people. This model is doomed if an agency is striving for financial sustainability. An agency must prioritize the core business based on the demands of the customer and the programs and services that generate the most revenue. Provide programs and services that are priorities for the community, and contract or partner for programs and services less demanded by the public. Meaning, the community can still be served, but outsource less profitable programs and services. The community is still served, and the agency uses the resources available to support the highest customer demand. The customer satisfaction in the community will build relationships, and building relationships will foster the third C, community advocacy.

Community Advocacy

A public sector agency has the benefit of using the "power of voices." The more an agency connects with the customer, the more fans the agency can acquire. An agency with a satisfied constituency base and market penetration of over 60% can be a powerful voice to elected officials. More importantly, the satisfied customer becomes a loyal fan and the voice for public support for parks and recreation services. Building advocacy is staying connected to your customer through superior customer service, quality products, and unwavering commitment to the ultimate parks and recreation experience.

The three Cs are really a continuum of connection to the community. The successful execution of one C will drive the others. Financial sustainability comes from attention to all three.

Mastering the 3 Cs is going to be critical for the growth and development of park and recreation in the environment of the "new normal." And with the skills and approaches taught at the NRPA Revenue Development and Management School, every agency can improve its position in its community, but building a more enterprise-focused agency and at the same time building the community and political support that need to go hand in hand with the expanded enterprise operations.

8

Partnering

Achieving Efficiencies With Strategic Partners

One of the mental obstacles that most organizations and individuals face is that we think we need to do everything ourselves. This perspective is inherently limiting. Even an organization as large as the federal government is going to be limited if it does not think beyond its own resources. And the larger the organization is, the more likely it will believe that it can and should do everything itself.

As you think about how to achieve the goals of your organization, the focus should first be on the end result that you want to achieve and only second on how the goal that is to be achieved. With the end goal in mind, think about what is the most efficient way to see the end result achieved. This open perspective, in which the method of achieving the goal is second to the end result, will allow you to consider a wider range of options.

There are always more resources available to help meet your mission if you are willing to look outside your organization and

let go of a little CONTROL.

Any goal can be achieved in multiple ways. It is often easier to think about the internal option where you do everything within your organization. It is easier because there is a high level of control of the process. But control should not be the goal, the end result is the proper goal, and control only serves to limit options.

Partnering comes from working with another organization that has overlapping goals with your own. When this happens, you can help them and they can help you. Partnerships can take many different forms from highly informal to highly formalized. Some of the options are discussed below.

Contracting With a Company that Has Expertise in the Area You Need

This is done all the time for services large and small, but the core of the relationship is a partnership. If the contractor has inherent efficiencies of scale, equipment, or expertise, they offer you elements that you would not be able to create internally as efficiently.

Partnering With Agencies that Offer a Very Similar Range of Products/Services

While on one level, another organization that is in the same business seems like a perfect partner, on the other hand it might have a higher likelihood of being a competitor. The best way to partner with such organizations is to have very well-defined projects and roles. Spelling out early the objectives and individual roles in the relationship/project can help two agencies that might otherwise be competitive say focused on the partnership.

While relationships with organizations that overlap can be more challenging in some ways, good partnerships are always worth pursuing.

Nonprofits

Nonprofits can be one of the best kinds of organization to partner with. This is because most nonprofits are mission driven. They know the end results they want to achieve and they rarely have the internal re-

sources (money, people, etc.) to fully achieve these goals. Because of this, they are more likely than other potential partners to actually want to work at working with others, and not trying to do everything themselves.

Friends Groups

Friends groups are organizations that are set up specifically to support a certain park, facility, or group of facilities with a common mission. Sometimes these can take the form of incorporated nonprofits, or sometimes they are unincorporated groups of volunteers. Because friends groups are organized around a mission to support a given facility, they are generally wonderful partners. Friends groups can raise funds for facilities or programs and/or be a source of volunteer help.

Volunteers

Volunteers generally need to be directed to tasks that they will like to do. Individuals and organizations that love the educational elements of your mission might well give of their time to help implement your educational goals. An environmental nonprofit may welcome the opportunity to enhance wildlife habitat on a property, just as a sports league might be willing to volunteer time and effort to maintain athletic fields. These kinds of partnerships are very common because they work so well.

A great way to encourage volunteerism is to treat it seriously. Give volunteers roles that are meaningful. A group showing up for a one-day work project might be limited to physical labor, but an individual who is willing to show up regularly can be treated more like a staff person and be given higher levels of responsibility. People volunteer in exchange for feeling good about their work and the difference they are making, so honoring them with recognition and awards can be effective (depending on their personality type). Put out periodic news releases about how many volunteer hours have been contributed to your organization. Highlight a group or individual who have made a great difference. Such marketing will make current volunteer feel good, and attract new ones.

Quid Pro Quo (Trade) Partnerships

Unlike truly donated time and effort without trade-in services, another model is that of barter of services for time and effort. Just as the athletic league will maintain fields if they get to use those fields, there are many other similar relationships. Some golfers will donate time to serve as course marshals or other workers at a golf course in exchange for so much free golf. Some people will serve as camp hosts, exchanging so many hours of work at a campground in exchange for a free campsite for their RV. So long as the services exchanged are of comparable value, such quid pro quo arrangements can be a good form of partnership. The organization achieves a need without a cash cost and builds loyalty in the process.

Creating partnerships and developing them is a time-consuming but rewarding task. While there might not be a cash cost to partnering with other groups or volunteers, there is a time cost to developing these relationships. Key steps in this process include the following:

- **Spend time in dialogue with potential partners.** It is only through dialogue that both parties can understand where they have overlapping goals that can create mutual benefit.
- **Recognize and appreciate your partners.** Make sure volunteers know how much they are appreciated and give public praise to partnering organizations. These steps will ensure that your partners will want to continue to find common ground with you.
- **Seek out new partners all the time.** Look and see who in your community is doing good work. Those are the organizations and individuals you want to attract to work with you.
- **Expand your self-limited options.** For every major objective, force your team to think of at least five totally different ways to achieve that goal. Option one may be the unimaginative "hire someone to do this." By the time you get to option three or four, you might be thinking about other resources that are currently in your community that you can partner with to achieve the goal. Remember: You can only achieve what you can envision, so thinking in a more expansive manner is the first step to great results.

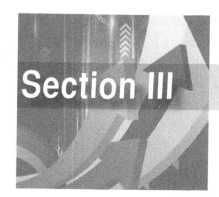

Human Resources

Have the Right People in the Right Positions

It may sound glib, but an organization is only as strong as the people who make up the group. Great advantages or disadvantages in facilities, market conditions and other factors can be overcome in either direction by the performance of the people in an organization. This makes human resources the most central of all resources.

Because of this dynamic, having the right people in the right positions and the wrong people away from where they can do harm is so important. While there is a lot written about hiring the right people, and we will cover more of this a little later, there is not a lot about the other side of having the wrong people in places where they will impede the performance of the organization. The reason this is not discussed much is that this dynamic is one of the most difficult for any organization to deal with. Too often, unproductive people are pushed to the sidelines and ignored rather than working to reengage these people or otherwise improve their performance.

General George Marshall

In 1939, when General George Marshall became Army Chief of Staff, everyone knew that it was only

General George Marshall

a matter of a short time before the world be engulfed by World War II. Marshall knew that the U.S. military was not ready for this challenge, and he set about getting the military ready. He did this first by removing those who were not helping the organization move forward. From 1939 to 1941, Marshall removed over 600 senior officers from their positions because they were not up to the task. These officers were not thrown away, they were put in other positions that seemed to align with their strengths better. In time, many were given other opportunities to lead.

Once the U.S. was in the war, the pattern continued with anyone who was not performing being reassigned in favor of those who had the qualities to win. In 1939, as training and preparations were in high swing, Marshall wanted all new training manuals ready in no less than four months. The Brigadier General in charge of this said it would take 18 months. When this person would not change his mind, Marshall relieved him of his duty and put someone in place who could get the job done. For some, this may seem hard-nosed and intolerant, but if the mission of the organization is important, then performance must be given top priority. The other issue is you are not doing a misaligned employee a favor by keeping him or her in a position the employee is unlikely to be happy in or good at. Help employees find a role that fits their talents and interests and employees and the organization both win.

Earlier in Marshall's career, he had listed the qualities he thought were critical to being a successful leader. His list included the following:

- Good common sense
- Having studied the profession
- Physically strong
- Cheerful and optimistic
- Display marked energy
- Extremely loyal
- Determined

The result of quickly removing people who were obstacles to success and, at the same time, promoting those who showed the can-do optimistic attitude that leads to success is why the U.S. Army soon earned a world-wide reputation as an adaptable learning organization. German Field Marshall Erwin Rommel, who was in charge of German Forces fighting the Americans in North Africa, said of the U.S. Army, "Astonishing … the speed with which the Americans adapted themselves."

The U.S. Army at the time was not the most technically advanced, but it overcame that obstacle by having some of the best leadership. Dwight Eisenhower was a Lt. Colonel in 1939, but by war's end, he was Commander of all Allied Forces in Europe. This only occurred because great talent was being promoted and weak performers were being removed on a regular basis. This meritocracy yielded great results.

Helping People Achieve Their Best

The golden rule tells us to treat others like we would like to be treated. If you were in a job that you were not good at, or were not happy and motivated in, it would not be kind to leave you in that position without trying to address the root issues. If a supervisor was not good at their job, it would not be kind to leave people under that person's direction. Often issues of people not performing well are avoided. They are avoided because we all would rather not have conflict, and sometimes the issues are avoided because we think it would be unkind to address problems in performance. In truth it may be unkind to not address these issues. We want people to be fulfilled in the knowledge that they are great at what they do. If they have the internal motivation, focus and skills they will feel good about themselves and others will feel good about working with them. In this way doing good personnel management can and should be an act of helping people to be their best.

An organization where people are held to high standards, employees are aligned with their skills and aptitudes, training is provided, and when there are performance issues they are addressed pro-actively way is exactly the kind of place most people would want to work. Such an organization is going to achieve great things as the talents of the individuals are released to help achieve the mission. The other interesting thing about holding people to high standards is that you are communicating that you believe that they are capable of achieving those standards. This is a compliment, and a challenge.

On the eve of a massive world war, General Marshall was given great authority and support to reassign and promote those who could make the organization into a high performance operation. From his example, we can see the great benefit of this approach. While in a modern HR environment, more documentation and process will be necessary, we should understand that getting the right people in the right places is absolutely key to making a high performance organization, and that it is not unkind to boldly address personnel issues that might be easier to avoid. If through good personnel management you can help people find where they can best contribute to the good of the organization you will be helping those people as well as those around them have a fulfilling work-life.

Individual Differences

Why Are Some People So Different?

How Do You Manage Such People?

Before we get into hiring, we need to examine individual differences, which will affect the way we look at whom we hire, how we communicate and make decisions, how we can most effectively work in teams, and much more.

There are a number of well-known personality tools that can help you get a handle on your personality and others. These tools can help any group know better what the strengths of different individuals are and how to use the diversity of the group to build a stronger entity.

The idea that people come hardwired differently is not universally known. Most of us wonder why some people act and think so differently. It is easy to get frustrated that others do not seem to see the world the way we do. Because we are right, of course! Without understanding individual differences, it is all too easy to look for others just like us to fill every position, because we understand and value our own personality type. If this is done, it can lead to catastrophic effects. Because in the end, a group is

> Unlocking the potential of individuals by
> aligning them with their strengths
>
> ## can create AMAZING results.

stronger if people use their best strengths, and different positions require different strengths.

The science of understanding individual differences should make us all feel a little less sure that all those others who are not like us are somehow wrong. In truth, we and they are all just different. Understanding our own profiles in one or more of the popular personality tests, can help us to be more understanding of who we are and why others see the world differently.

In this chapter, we will look at Meyers-Briggs, Herrmann Whole Brain Model, and Strengthfinder 2.0 tests. There are other excellent personality tools, but because they all play a similar role in showing the areas where you function best and are most comfortable, looking at these three popular models will give us an accurate picture.

From the perspective of the individual, understanding your personality with one of these models can help you understand your strengths and build on them. From the perspective of managing or leading a group, the understanding of what an individual's strengths are can help you make sure that the person with the right aptitude is in the right position. It can also help to organize groups of people with complementary (but not the same) skills. Such teams working on common issues with members that bring different perspectives and skills can be very powerful. Their ability to perform well is also enhanced when the members of the team know that they all have different personality profiles. This will enhance the tolerance and understanding they all have, and keep the inevitable different perspectives from becoming conflicts.

Meyers-Briggs

Meyers-Briggs is one of the oldest and best known personality type tools (see Figure 9.1). It was developed in the 1940s and is based on Jungian psychology. It uses a four letter signature to describe where people get their energy from, how information is gathered about the world, how they process that information, and how they come to closure on their decisions. From these four characteristics, a great deal of insight can be drawn about the personality of an individual and how he or she will work and interact with others.

The Myers-Briggs™ Type Indicator
(The Keirsey Temperament Sorter)

E Extroverted (Expressive)	**S** Sensing (Observant)	**T** Thinking (Tough-minded)	**J** Judging (Scheduling)
I Introverted (Reserved)	**N** Intuitive (Introspective)	**F** Feeling (Friendly)	**P** Perceiving (Probing)

Figure 9.1. Myers-Briggs Elements

Extroverted/Introverted

Extroverted/introverted has more to do with where people get their energy than if they can be a fun person at a party. We can all engage in social interactions, and we can all engage in quiet study. However, the extrovert will be energized by the group social interaction, and the introvert will be energized by the time spent in quiet study. From an employment perspective, the extrovert might be a good choice for someone who will be in nearly constant interaction with customers. Introverts might do just as good a job at this, but it would be draining to them. On the other hand, someone who is going to be a grant writer and researcher might be better suited to the job if he or she is an introvert. That person might love the time spent researching and writing and gain energy from that environment. Here again, an extrovert might do an excellent job as the grant writer, but might need more distractions that allow for social time.

Intuitive/Sensing

Intuitive/sensing has to do with where people get their information about the world. The intuitive person is going to be more prone to thinking strategically about the future and creating innovations. This is because this type thinks in big-picture abstractions and less in the details. These people might be great at creating new and exciting programs and helping the organization reach new and unforeseen heights.

The sensing person is much more focused on the details he can sense in front of him; what he sees, hears, or can touch. As such, these people are very grounded in the here and now. Both forms of collecting information have their value. You need the intuiters to help keep the organization fresh, relevant, and forward focused, and you need the sensing people to keep the details straight, and everything well organized. In the farmer vs. Viking analogy, the sensing persons are the farmers focused on what is right in front of them and their fields to manage, and the Vikings are the intuiters who are looking to the future and seeing new opportunities.

Feeling/Thinking

Feeling/thinking has to do with how you process the information. Feelers focus first on the human impact of any situation or relationships. These people might be very well suited to working with others since they are looking to foster good relationships.

The thinkers process their information on a much cooler, logical basis, without putting peoples' feelings as the top priority. These people are very good at making rational decisions.

I saw the difference of thinkers vs. feelers recently during a discussion among a number of parks and recreation officials at a conference. One person said that our field is only as strong as our people, and that a big issue we needed to focus on was how we are going to keep benefits strong so we know we are taking good care of our people. This man presented a classic feeler's response to the issues. Another person assertively said that

she totally disagreed and that for every job there was a line of other qualified people ready to take the place of current employees; if they didn't like
the benefits, they could leave. You could sense the tension in the room. The
second person was very clearly a thinker on the Meyers-Briggs model; she
was logical. On one level she was absolutely right; there are always many
qualified job applicants, so it is not the end of the world when someone
leaves a job. But the statement showed no preference for the people side
of the equation, and the direct confrontation of the first person's comment
showed no value for that person's "feeling" in that moment.

The feeling person might be great at building a strong, loyal team, because she cares a great deal about the people. However, the thinker is
going to give you the clear-eyed truth about the situation—a truth that is
backed up by logic and facts. You probably need both perspectives in a
high performance organization. Being blind to either side will not work.

Perceiving/Judging

Perceiving/judging is the difference in how fast and firm decisions are
made. A person who is a perceiver is open minded and not quick to come
to judgment. This can be a positive and endearing quality but can also lead
to indecision and delay. The judger will use his thinking or feeling decision
making and come to judgment quickly and decisively. This can be highly
effective in getting things done but might lead to rash decisions based on
too little information.

Gender differences exist within the Meyers-Briggs profiles, and some
combinations of personality characteristics are much more common than
others. One of the main differences is that women are much more inclined
to be feelers in their decision making, and men are much more likely to be
thinkers in theirs. While this difference often falls along gender lines, anyone can be any profile, and in the scenario described above, it was a wom-
an showing the thinking dominance and a man showing the feeling dominance. Figure 9.2 shows the various combinations on the Meyers-Briggs
model and what careers fit with these profiles.

Popular Career Choices by Type

ISTJ (14%) Take Your Time and Do It Right	ISFJ (11%) On My Honor, To Do My Duty	INFJ (2%) Catalyst for Positive Change	INTJ (3%) Competence + Independence=Perfection
Steelworker	Physician: Family, GP	Psychologist / Psychiatrist	Computer Programmer
Veterinarian	Dietician / Nutritionist	Clergy	College Professor
Police / Detective	Teacher: Preschool, Elem.	Novelist / Playwright	Chemical Engineer
Accountant / Auditor	Guidance Counselor	Human Resources	Lawyer / Judge
Manager / Administrator	Librarian	Teacher: English/Drama	Architect
Military Officer	Nurse	Educational Consultant	Scientist:
Engineering Technician	Optician	Social Worker	Management Consultant
Efficiency Analyst	Clerical Supervisor	Mediator	Strategic Planner
Estate Planner	Probation Officer	Speech Pathologist	Investment Banker
ISTP (6%) Doing the Best with What I've Got	**ISFP (6%)** It's the Thought That Counts	**INFP (4%)** Still Waters Run Deep	**INTP (5%)** Ingenious Problem Solvers
Farmer	Administrative Assistant	Minister / Priest	Researcher
Construction Worker	Fashion Designer	Musician / Composer	Computer Programmer
Pilot	Chef	Psychologist / Psychiatrist	Chemist / Biologist
Computer Specialist	Physical Therapist	HR Development	Lawyer
Banker	Beautician	Educational Consultant	Financial Planner
Intelligence Agent	Landscape Designer	Social Worker / Counselor	Mathematician
Park Ranger	Storekeeper / Clerk	Writer / Editor / Reporter	Technical Consultant
Engineer	Dental Assistant	Artist / Entertainer	Artist / Photographer
Police / Security	Bookkeeper	Teacher: Special Ed, Art	College Professor
ESTP (6%) Let's Get Busy!	**ESFP (7%)** Don't Worry, Be Happy!	**ENFP (7%)** Anything's Possible	**ENTP (5%)** Life's Entrepreneurs
Paramedic / Firefighter	Lifeguard / Rec. Attendant	Journalist	Politician
Pro Athlete	Child Care Worker	Character Actor	Sales Manager
Auditor	Sales Representative	Marketing Consultant	Venture Capitalist
Field Sales Rep	Travel Agent	Advertising Director	Systems Analyst
Optometrist	Receptionist / Secretary	Corporate Trainer	Market Researcher
Marketing Professional	Promoter / Fund-Raiser	Teacher: Drama / Music	Strategic Planner
Promoter	Respiratory Therapist	Counselor / Psychologist	Management Consultant
Stockbroker	Film Producer	Musician / Composer	Advertising Director
General Contractor	Waiter / Waitress	Photographer	Newscaster / Reporter
ESTJ (11%) Taking Care Of Business	**ESFJ (11%)** What Can I Do For You?	**ENFJ (4%)** The Public Relations Specialist	**ENTJ (4%)** Everything's Fine – I'm in Charge
Teacher: Trade/Technical	Nurse / Phys. Therapist	Writer / Journalist	Executive / CEO
Project Manager	Pediatric Medicine	Psychologist / Counselor	Investment Broker
School Administrator	Teacher: K-12	Clergy / Priest	Business Consultant
Factory Supervisor	Retail Owner / Operator	Entertainer / Actor	Attorney / Judge
Executive	Athletic Coach	Marketing / Public Relations	Sales Manager
Military Officer	Flight Attendant	Recruiter	Credit Investigator
Public Official	Hairdresser	Trainer / Consultant	Marketing Personnel
Bank Officer	Office Manager	Teacher: College	Computer Professional
Insurance Agent	Home Economist	Physician: Family, GP	Franchise Owner

Remember: All 16 types can be successful in any profession.

Figure 9.2. Meyers-Briggs Career Choices

Herrmann Whole Brain Model

The whole brain model is fascinating because it correlates very well to the Meyers-Briggs model (Figure 9.3) but was developed in a completely different way. When real-time brain imaging technology became available, we were able to see that different areas of the brain are busiest when we are thinking in different ways.

This model breaks areas of the brain into four quadrants. Through a questionnaire, this model can plot the areas of the brain where dominance is highest and lowest. If you score high in the lower right, you most likely would be a feeler on the Meyers-Briggs, and if you are strong in the upper right, you most likely are intuitive. Upper left would fit with a thinker on Meyers-Briggs, and the lower left would most likely be a sensing person.

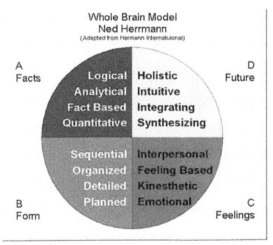

Figure 9.3. Hermann Whole Brain Model

Strengthfinder 2.0

The Gallup Organization developed Strengthfinder 2.0 based on over 40 years of survey data. The result is a simple online test that gives you a profile of strengths based on 34 common strengths (Figure 9.4). Many of the books published by Gallop, including *Now, Discover Your Strengths, Strengthfinder 2.0, Strengths-Based Leadership,* and others, have a code in the book that at allow you to access this online tool. Like the other person-

Figure 9.4. Common Strengths Profiled in Strengthfinder 2.0

ality tests, this can be a useful tool in understanding what you are best at so you can focus your efforts in those areas.

Whether you use Herrmann Whole Brain, Meyers-Briggs, or another of the good personality tests out there, including Strengthfinder 2.0, the challenge is to improve the performance of an organization with this knowledge. Following are some general guidelines.

Put the Right People in the Right Places

Author and management consultant Jim Collins wrote in his book, *Good to Great,* that one of the keys to success was "getting the right people on the bus, the wrong people off the bus, and the right people in the right seats." Getting the right people into the organization and in the right positions requires some insights into individual differences. We all function best when we are building off our natural skills and aptitude. Because of this, if you need to hire someone to be in charge of finances, you want to look for someone who is highly analytical, with a good eye for details, and if you want to hire someone who can sell your product or service, you will want someone who is naturally extroverted and can engage strangers with ease.

What this means is that in addition to the list of skill sets that you may define in a job description, you also want to talk to the team that will be doing the interviews and hiring of a position about the personality type you are looking for, and what to look for in order for a candidate to fit the organizational culture of the group.

Diverse Teams

Most people like others who are a lot like they are, people with similar personality types. While others like you might make great friends, having all people who think alike is not a great formula for success. The reason is that to achieve organizational goals and mission, you will need skill sets in a variety of areas, and if you hire all people who are like you, your group might be blind to important issues that a different personality type could easily identify and address.

Great teams have a few things in common, including the following:

- Complementary skills (not the same)
- Common purpose (mission)
- Collective accountability (reporting)

So the team members have a common mission and common reporting, but they have had different skills that they bring to the task. Think of almost any sports team, where players will specialize in different positions based on their unique skills.

Teams of Generals

An Example of Using Individual Strengths to Build Strong Teams

During the American Civil War, both sides had a winning team of generals with a winning combination of personality types.

For the South, the winning combination was Robert E. Lee, who was a great strategic big-picture thinker; J.E.B. Stuart, who was very charismatic and adept

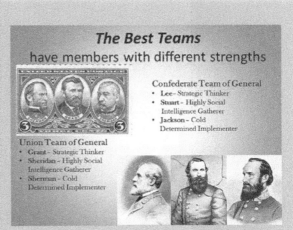

The Best Teams
have members with different strengths

Confederate Team of General
- Lee - Strategic Thinker
- Stuart - Highly Social Intelligence Gatherer
- Jackson - Cold Determined Implementer

Union Team of General
- Grant - Strategic Thinker
- Sheridan - Highly Social Intelligence Gatherer
- Sherman - Cold Determined Implementer

at gaining battlefield intelligence; and Thomas "Stonewall" Jackson, who was a relentless implementer of the strategy and would stop for nothing.

For the North, there was a successful team made up of the same mix of personality types. Ulysses S. Grant was the strategist, Phillip Sheridan was the charismatic intelligence gatherer, and William T. Sherman was the relentless implementer.

Both of these teams were very successful because they brought together complementary skills and personality types.

The most successful teams consist of individuals with complementary skills.

Hiring the Best

The very first task in hiring employees is to decide if you really need that position to achieve your goals. This step is most often missed when filling a vacant position after someone has left. There often is an assumption that because you used to have someone doing that job that the position must be filled to continue your operations. In reality, there are probably multiple ways of achieving the goals. You could contract out some of the functions, you might be able to realign job responsibilities in a way that shares this role with several other existing employees. Or maybe on examination that function does not need to be done at all. The point of these questions is that before the job is advertised, do some analysis to determine if the job needs to be filled, and if it does, is there a better way of doing it? Only after these issues have been answered are you ready to advertise an open position. Since personnel costs are generally the highest cost in most organizations, the decisions about staffing are critical to the success of the organization.

If you have determined that you need a new employee, the next step is to advertise the position, and to do this you need a good job description. Often, there is a previous job description that was used in the past. It is almost better not to look at the old description until you have outlined what you think the current requirements of the job are. Perhaps the old description was not well written, or perhaps the job has evolved since the last time a position like this was advertised. Either way, a fresh approach will likely produce a better end result. Defining the job has two elements, the tangible requirements and the abstract ones.

Tangible Requirements Include:

- Primary Responsibilities—what they will do
  - Hours
  - Pay and benefits
- Education
- Experience:
  - Industry vs. functional
  - Large organization vs. small

Abstract requirements include:

- Personality characteristics
  - Analytical or creative abilities
- Decision making style
- Interpersonal skills and style
- Organizational culture

The tangible requirements will be included in the written job description that will be advertised to people inside and outside the organization. The abstract requirements or preferences are important to discuss and have some agreement on your interview team so you can look for these preferred characteristics among the job candidates.

One of the biggest questions in the hiring process is "Do you need to hire someone with excellent experience doing the exact job you want to fill?" Or should you hire someone with the right aptitude who shows a willingness to learn the new job? Most employers' first reaction is that they want the experienced "pro" who has done a job just like this in the past. While this experienced "pro" may be able to hit the ground running and not need much or any training, there are positives and negatives to each type of candidates.

Less experienced but willing and able to learn:

Pros

- Learns the way you like to do things.
- Might have greater loyalty to the organization.
- Lower potential income level.

Cons

- It takes time to train them and get employee up to speed.
- There is risk in making the investment.

More experienced "pro" at this job:

Pros

- Can do the job right away without much training.
- Brings potentially helpful experience from previous job doing the same thing.

Cons

- Might bring old habits that might not be the way you would like to do business.
- Will most likely come at a higher cost than the less experienced person.

There is no one right answer as to whether to hire the less experienced person with the right aptitudes, or the more experienced person. Each could be a good hire, but each comes with pros and cons.

The case for the less experienced person was well expressed by Herb Kelleher, the former CEO of Southwest Airlines, when he said:

> If you don't have a good attitude, we don't want you,
> no matter how skilled you are.
> We can change skill levels through training.
>
> *We can't change attitude.*

Southwest Airlines put the abstract quality of a good attitude and friendly demeanor ahead of all the tangible attributes in a new employee. Because of this strategy, Southwest quickly became a commercial success in a highly competitive industry. They understood that the attitude of their employees was the most important factor in providing a great customer experience. And they understood that the detailed skills of any of the jobs could be taught to the person with the right attitude. This approach increases your training costs and time, but has great advantages over just hiring people based on experience.

A job description that will help you attract the right candidate should include the following elements: Having the mission of the organization as part of the job description may attract good candidates who otherwise would not seek out that job, and may discourage some who would not be motivated by your mission. Understanding where in the organizational structure this job fits will help the resourceful job candidate in the interview to have a better understanding of who he or she will report to and how his or her skills can help both the organization and the direct supervisor. Characteristics required to do a good job get to the Southwest model where they were looking for friendly people to interact with the public.

- Include elements of the mission culture and goals of the organization
- Job title
- Responsibilities and tasks
- Where the position fits in the structure (reporting)
- Compensation, hours, location
- Characteristics required to do a good job

While there is often a desire to promote from within an organization, the best policy is always to hire the best possible candidate for the job, wherever he or she comes from. This policy keeps everyone on their toes. It also lets everyone know that they are expected to be at the top of their game if they are going to be promoted. As a manager, one of your jobs is to mentor and train those who report to you, so that they are ready to advance when and if the opportunity arises. You would like your internal candidate to compare well with the best the industry has to offer, but it is important to be willing to fill the position with an outside candidate if one appears to be the best option.

The channels for advertising an open position can include some mix of the following avenues:

- Targeted job websites
- General job websites
- Posting the job offering on the company's website
- Newspaper ads (circulation of many papers are declining)
- Trade publications
- Professional associations
- Referrals and personal networks
- Job fairs

The next step in the process will be screening the resumes that come in for the open position. In many cases, you can have an enormous stack of resumes to review. If so, the first step is to cut the pile into the ones that look promising enough for a more detailed examination and those that do not make the cut. Some of the things to look for include the following:

- Signs of performance/results
- Career goal and progression that fit this position
- Employment gaps
- Pattern of employment
- Logical progression
- Too long-winded

Of these items, the candidate's ability to convey some successes/results is a great sign that the person is results-oriented. If the resume and cover letter are

"My short-term goal is to bluff my way through this job interview. My long-term goal is to invent a time machine so I can come back and change everything I've said so far."

Copyright 2002 by Randy Glasbergen

too long and overly detailed, it may be an indication that this person has difficulty focusing on priorities.

A new trend that seems to be growing is to have potential job candidates take a personality test prior to being selected for an interview. The Society for Human Resource Management believes that about 18% of companies are taking this approach, and that number is growing. The advantages of requiring a Meyers-Briggs or Herrmann Whole Brain test is that it would give the interview team a better indication of aptitude than you could easily get from an interview alone.

Interview

When hiring a full-time employee, it is best to have more than one interviewer. This provides a variety of perspectives on how well the interview went, and it also protects the interviewers by having a witness.

There are a number of questions that cannot be legally asked such as issues of the candidate's age, sexual orientation, children, or disabilities that cannot influence the hiring decision. Those questions include the following:

- How old are you (unless you are hiring a youth that might not be old enough to work)?
- Are you married?
- What is your sexual orientation?
- How much do you weigh?
- Are you disabled?
- When did you graduate from high school?
- Do you have children?
- Where were you born?
- What religion are you?
- Other related questions

As an interview team, it is best to collectively come up with a set of questions that you think will get at some of the tangible and abstract issues that will determine success in this position. Agree ahead of time who will ask what questions, and use the same set of questions with each candidate so you have points of comparison.

Some of the most common questions that interviewers ask include the following:

- Tell us about your educational and employment background and how this will help you succeed in this position.
- What do you know about "X" agency?
- Why are you attracted to "X" agency and this position?
- What are your strengths?
- What are your weaknesses?
- What are your career goals?
- Define your leadership style.
- Why are you the best candidate?
- Do you have questions for us?

The problem with standard questions is that most job candidates will have prepared answers for these. This might not give you the best insights into the candidate. Create your own questions that relate to the position. One of the standard questions that is not recommended is "What are your weaknesses?" This question about weaknesses will rarely be answered honestly and fails to focus on the more important issue of what are this person's best strengths.

Keeping and Training the Best

Healthy organizations have a balance of retention and turnover. If no one leaves the organization, there are few opportunities for others to move up, and the organization can get stale and lack the energy that comes from new people and new ideas. On the other side, if too many people leave, you can lose institutional knowledge and productivity. It can be demoralizing to see too many people leaving an organization.

Most organizations have a 10% to 30% turnover on an annual basis. When the number of people leaving gets too high, the following negative side effects can happen.

- Loss in productivity
- Need to hire and train a new person
- Negative effect on morale; others might think of leaving
- Loss of average employees costs the organization 1/3 of their salary
- Loss of a good senior employee costs 2 to 3 times employee's salary
- Turnover affects customer service, which affects the bottom line

Why employees choose to stay at an organization is that most or all the pieces of the circle of satisfaction are in place (Figure 11.1). Each element of this circle reinforces a person's job satisfaction and willingness to continue with that employer.

Figure 11.1. Circle of Satisfaction

Just as there is a circle of satisfaction, there is also a circle of dissatisfaction that will lead employees to seek employment elsewhere (Figure 11.2). Each of these circles feeds off the other and creates either an upward or downward spiral. As an employer, the goal needs to be to facilitate the elements in the satisfaction circle, and try to minimize the elements in the circle of dissatisfaction.

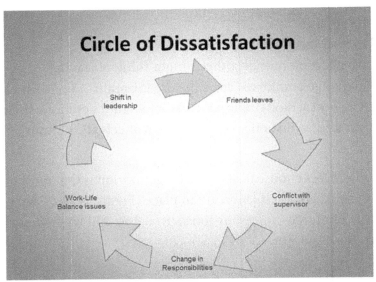

Figure 11.2. Circle of Dissatisfaction

Not all employee turnover has an equal impact on an organization. An employee who has not been employed long might not have a significant impact upon departure. An employee with poor work habits—or worse, a bad attitude—can actually boost morale and productivity if he or she leaves.

The most important type of employees to keep fall into the following categories:

- **Provide leadership.** This can be formal leadership on the organizational chart or informal opinion leaders.
- **Consistently achieve excellent results.** Keep those with great productivity and good judgment.
- **Contribute new and innovative ideas.** Some people are significantly more creative than others, and it is important to keep enough creative people around to keep the organization on the leading edge of the field.
- **Require little or no supervision.** People who know their jobs well and are self-starters are of great value.
- **Facilitate the work of others.** You need people who are great team players and help provide the informal leadership.
- **Information "nodes" within the organization.** People who easily form connections with people in other departments, organizations, partners, and/or customers are vital information nodes within an organization and worth more than just the official job they perform.
- **Unique knowledge or skills.** Specialized or technical knowledge is always of high value.

How Important Is Money?

Generally, compensation is less important than many people assume. If the elements of the circle of satisfaction are in place, it is likely that most people will be happy to stay. Where compensation does come into play is if it is perceived as unfair. This perception can happen if many other similar organizations are paying significantly more for the same skill set, or if the employee feels unappreciated. 20th century psychologist Frederick Herzberg found that intrinsic motivators, like mission, recognition, and sense of progress, were more important to employee satisfaction than extrinsic factors such as compensation. Another workplace psychologist, John Stacey Adam, found in his "equity theory" that perceived fairness of any compensation system was critical to employee satisfaction.

So, if it is not money, what is the number one motivator of employees?

Progress

In their book, *The Progress Principle*, psychologists Teresa Amabile and Steven Kramer illustrate how a sense of progress at work is the most important single factor to job satisfaction. People long to see how their efforts are leading to positive results, and when that feedback can be in place, the results are powerful.

So, for organizational managers, one of the important tasks is to hold up organizational achievements for all to see, and to recognize individual contributions to build a sense of positive momentum for both the individuals and the organization.

Relationship With Supervisor

If progress is the most important factor to build job satisfaction, the relationship of the employee with the direct supervisor is the most single important factor that predicts if an employee will choose to stay or go. If you look again at the circle of satisfaction and the circle of discontent, you will notice that on the first, "respected supervisor" was important for satisfaction, and on the second, "conflict with supervisor" was key to discontent. Sometimes personality conflicts are unavoidable; however, if one supervisor is experiencing higher than average turnover, it might be the sign of a supervisor who is consistently in conflict with his or her employees.

For any supervisor, the balance of the relationship with employees is an interesting challenge. You do not want to be their best personal friend, or it can be difficult to review them objectively and hold them accountable for results. On the other side, you do not want to be perceived as unfair or unkind. Creating that positive relationship with productive feedback, positive reinforcement, and professional detachment, is something some people are better at than others. If you are going to keep your most talented and productive employees, having well-trained and mentored supervisors is your best single tool.

Some of the things a supervisor can do to build healthy relationships with employees are as follows:

- Always strive to be fair.
- Treat everyone in an impartial way.
- Communicate clear goals and objectives.
- Focus on results, not details.
- Provide the resources employees need for success.
- Celebrate performance, progress, and success.

Some strategies for building an organization with healthy retention include the following:

- Hire the best to begin with.
- Develop a good supervisor/employee relationship.
- Share information—strategy, financial, and goals—to demonstrate trust and respect for employees.
- Give them as much autonomy and responsibility as they can handle.
- Challenge them to meet new heights.
- Be flexible on work-life balance issues.
- Recognize and reward excellence.

12

Performance-Based Review and Compensation

Employee reviews and pay systems should be seen as integral to the larger goal of building a high performance organization. They are arguably the most important parts of any organizational development effort. Ideally, you want every employee to know what his or her role is in achieving the larger organizational goals. You want to have a clear way to measure success. And you want incentives in place to motivate the individual actions that will lead to success. In a perfect world, if all of these systems are in place and working well, your need to manage people will be minimal—essentially setting goals—because everyone will be self-motivated to do all the right things.

As former General Electric CEO Jack Welch said,

> If you pick the right people and give them the opportunity to spread their wings and put compensation as a carrier behind it,
>
> ### *you almost don't have to manage them.*

The problem with most public sector review and compensation systems is that they are not good at measuring success or rewarding it.

Grade and Step Systems

A common system used in governments for many decades is grades and steps (see Figure 12.1). Each job position is assigned a grade (a numerical value), and within that grade are a number of steps. Each step is an opportunity to earn typically 3-5% more. On an annual basis (or sometimes every other year) the employee is reviewed by the supervisor and may be eligible for a step increase. While this is technically a merit system in that the supervisors do not need to grant the step increase, from a practical perspective, steps are usually granted unless there are significant performance issues. And, since the steps are a set percentage, a great employee and a mediocre one will get the same raise on the anniversary of their employment. So, great performers and mediocre performers move up the ladder at the same rate, based almost completely on years of service.

Grade & Step Salary System

Table below is from the Federal Government and is similar to most state and local government salary systems

Grade	Step 1	Step 2	Step 3	Step 4	Step 5	Step 6	Step 7	Step 8	Step 9	Step 10
1	20607	21295	21980	22662	23347	23750	24427	25110	25137	25779
2	23169	23720	24486	25137	25417	26164	26911	27658	28406	29153
3	25279	26122	26965	27807	28650	29492	30335	31178	32020	32863
4	28379	29325	30272	31219	32165	33112	34058	35005	35951	36898
5	31751	32808	33866	34924	35982	37039	38097	39155	40213	41271
6	35392	36572	37752	38931	40111	41291	42471	43651	44831	46011
7	39330	40641	41951	43262	44572	45883	47193	48503	49814	51124
8	43557	45009	46460	47912	49364	50816	52268	53720	55172	56624
9	48108	49712	51317	52921	54525	56129	57733	59338	60942	62546
10	52979	54745	56511	58277	60044	61810	63576	65342	67108	68875
11	58206	60146	62087	64027	65967	67908	69848	71788	73728	75669
12	69764	72090	74416	76742	79068	81394	83720	86046	88372	90698
13	82961	85727	88493	91259	94025	96791	99557	102323	105088	107854
14	98033	101301	104569	107836	111104	114372	117639	120907	124175	127442
15	115317	119161	123006	126850	130694	134538	138383	142227	146071	149000

* Rate limited to the rate for level IV of the Executive Schedule (5 U.S.C. 5304 (g)(1)).

Figure 12.1. Grade and Step Salary System

Common "Pay for Performance" Systems

Based on information from the International City Managers Association (ICMA), the primary systems that local governments are moving to in order to focus better on performance are "pay band systems" (see Figure 12.2).

Pay bands use a range of percentage increases that supervisors can pick from when conducting an annual performance review, rather than the single percentage value used in a step system. Such systems can be either effective or cost prohibitive, based on how well they are used by supervisors. The problem with most local government performance measures is that the goals are highly subjective and not measurable. Because of this, it is easier for supervisors to be overly generous in saying everyone is above average. The result of that is rapid escalation of the payroll. A variation of this system is known as "open range" and allows for great latitude on the part of the supervisor within a broad range set by the grade.

Pay Bands/Open Range

Pay bands or open range provide a minimum and maximum and the supervisor can pick what compensation within that range matches performance, and experience. This is different from Grade and Step that is driven by number of years on the job vs. performance.

*This example shows pay ranges in two market areas with different costs of living

SALARY RANGE WITH LOCALITY PAY				
	Washington, D.C. Metro Area		St. Louis, MO Metro Area	
Pay Band	Minimum	Maximum*	Minimum	Maximum*
01	$22,155	$57,690	$20,324	$53,018
02	$42,209	$77,708	$38,790	$71,415
03	$62,467	$121,677	$57,408	$111,823
04	$89,033	$143,785	$81,823	$132,140
05	$123,758	$155,550S	$113,735	$155,439

*Maximum includes equivalent of a step 12 derived from the former highest GS grade of Band.
**Maximum salary of Band 05 with locality pay may not exceed Level IV of the Executive Schedule plus 5%.

Figure 12.2. Pay Bands

There is currently a significant trend of governments looking for a more performance-based system of rewarding employees than has been the norm in the past. And a well-administered pay band or open-range system tied to measurable goals can be effective. But there is the risk of supervisors taking the easy route and giving social promotions.

Goals for Any Review and Reward System

While the primary goal of a reward system is to unleash new levels of productivity that will help the organization reach new heights and serve the community in new and better ways, a good system should have a number of other goals, including the following:

- Creating higher job satisfaction (motivation)
- Be seen as fair and equitable
- Be affordable for the agency over the long term
- Not to have such radical change from the previous system that it is disruptive and works counter to our other goals

Research on Incentive Systems

Frederick Herzberg, a psychologist who focused on what motivates employees, was one of the most influential thinkers in this area in the 20th century. Herzberg is most famous for pushing back on the popular theory that the more you paid people, the more motivated they would be. He found that intrinsic motivation (i.e., mission, recognition, sense of progress) was more powerful than extrinsic (money) motivation. None of this suggests that compensation was not important, it just was not the primary indicator of productivity and happiness. Herzberg did see money as an important symbol of recognition. He also pointed out that pay systems that did not seem fair and objective to employees could demotivate a group.

Another workplace psychologist, John Stacey Adam, proposed his equity theory. His theory also supports the idea that perceived fairness in any reward/compensation system is important. He also believed that employees tried to balance their inputs (work) to the level of rewards that the employer was offering. This theory would support the use of a highly quantifiable (objective) reward system, which would be seen as fair and would provide incentives for excellence.

Numerous quantitative studies and academic papers on the impact of incentive pay systems support the idea that such systems do drive higher productivity. Some of these are listed below:

- Dohmen, T., Falk, A., Institute of the Study of Labor in Bonn. (March 2006). *Performance Pay and Multidimensional Sorting: Productivity, Preferences, and Gender.*
  - Output was much higher for workers in variable pay schemes compared to fixed pay schemes.
  - Risk-averse workers preferred fixed pay schemes.

- Lavy, V., Hebrew University, RH University of London, NBER, and CEPR. (April 2008). *Performance Pay and Teachers' Effort, Productivity, and Grading Ethics*
  - 32% increase in math and 24% increase in English score in students taught by incentivized teachers.

- Risher, H. W., American Management Association, and American Compensation Association. (1999). *Aligning Pay and Results: Compensation Strategies that Work from the Boardroom to the Shop Floor.* New York: American Management.
  - Long-term success of companies correlates to employees being able to share in success.
  - It is always advantageous to align new pay programs with organizational goals.
  - In many organizations only higher level jobs are bonus eligible.
  - Aligning strategy, structure, systems, processes, staffing and culture create organizations that are designed to succeed

- Lazear, E. P., The American Economic Review. (December 2000). *Performance Pay and Productivity.*
  - A switch to piece-rate compensation scheme and 10% increase in overall compensation resulted in a 44% gain in productivity in a factory setting.

- Robertson, P. J., Seneviratne, S. J., Public Administration Review. (December 1995). *Outcomes of Planned Organizational Change in the Public Sector: A Meta-Analytic Comparison to the Private Sector.*
  - Analysis of 47 change initiatives found 84% of public sector efforts had positive outcomes, and 89% of privates sector initiatives generated positive outcomes.
  - Greatest challenge for many public sector changes is the lack of market incentives, conflicting goals, more layers of rules and regulations.

High Performance Review System

Where most governments lack clear goals and measurable results, which are key to an effective incentive program, the field of parks and recreation has a great potential to measure performance better than many other branches of government. From tracking number of program participants from year to year, to tracking the percentage of enterprise revenues per facility or per agency, there are good metrics to count. If an agency has a good strategic plan and business plan for each facility, these plans offer even more meaningful metrics to track. From goals like these, you can develop individual goals that all advance your strategic planning goals. If each individual is held personally accountable for important goal elements, and there is an objective review and reward connected to these goals, you have a high performance agency!

This level of accountability requires a lot of supervisors. Both supervisors and employees must understand that this detailed and objective list of individual goals will provide an objective measure of whether an individual employee has done what she/he needs to do to merit a raise or bonus. If the supervisor and employee agree in writing at the beginning of the year what the measurable results will be and put this into the personnel file for that employee, it will come as no surprise to either party what the measurable results will be.

Potential Performance Bonus System

Pay bands tend to inflate the overall payroll for an agency, and also drive up related expenses such as retirement benefits that are based on ending pay range. This can be potentially unsustainable for the organization.

Many parks and recreation agencies have an enterprise fund for all or most of their facilities. Enterprise funds are not supported by tax dollars. They are designed to allow governments to run some operations more like a business. One of the results of this is that at the end of the year, if there is "net revenue" (a profit in the private sector world), it stays in the enterprise fund and is not absorbed by the larger city/county/state general fund. Because enterprise funds are not supported with tax dollars, there is more freedom in how they are used.

This enterprise fund offers a unique opportunity for an incentive system. A set percentage of the net revenue from the enterprise fund could be designated for a bonus pool. This bonus pool will be different every year based on performance. In years of good financial performance, there will be a larger bonus pool, and in years of poor performance, there may be a small bonus pool or none. A bonus system based on this kind of fund will create an incentive for overall financial performance of the agency. This means there will be an incentive for everyone to both save on expenses, where possible, and bring in new revenue, where possible. So everyone will be pulling for the same goal, and there will not be the perception that all funds that are budgeted should be spent.

If the enterprise fund is used to create a bonus pool, it is advisable to have the bonus available to all full-time employees in the agency, whether their position is funded by the enterprise fund or the general fund. This would create the perceived fairness that Herzberg and Adams both thought was critical to a successful pay system.

A great advantage of a bonus system over an open-range system is that it will not inflate the overall payroll expense from year to year. Because a bonus based on a percentage of net revenue in the enterprise fund created a one-time incentive pay and not a long-term increase in salary, it is sustainable in good years and bad.

The advantages of this type of bonus system include the following:

- It would not adversely impact the agency in down economic conditions.
- It would not add to retirement liabilities because the bonus would not be calculated into final compensation.
- It would make all full-time employees feel like they own a stake in the organization.
- It would be highly fair and transparent.
- It is highly goal-oriented and measurable.
- It would provide incentives to those employees who are at "end of range" on the step system.

Whether a pay band system, open range, or bonus, it is advantageous to move past the old grade system as the only form of compensation. This bureaucratic pay system never measured performance and never rewarded great performance over mediocre performance. If you want to have a high performance agency, you need systems that measure and reward performance.

Systems ➤ Organizational Culture ➤ Performance

Disciplinary Action

When I have taught this class to undergraduate students, it becomes known as "how to fire people." This class is of great interest to the students, not so much because of the negative and dramatic nature of termination of employment, but because this is a subject that many people are curious about, and it is generally not taught very often.

Every organization has its own personnel policies. These policies usually spell out cause for termination and other disciplinary actions. Before taking any action as a supervisor of others, **read the personnel policy, and check with the human resources (personnel) department for guidance.** What is stated in this chapter is common practice in many work environments, but not all policies or practices are the same.

Unionized work places will have more regulations on such matters that will be part of collective bargaining agreements. In such environments, it is even more important to follow the letter of the regulation and be advised by human resources experts. The human resources department can help a supervisor understand when he can act and when management should consult with legal advisors.

THIS CHAPTER SHOULD NOT BE CONSTRUED AS LEGAL ADVICE.

We have discussed hiring the best, the key role of supervisors, how to be a mentoring boss, and how to focus on measurable results and accountability. But sometimes the best management techniques do not work, and disciplinary action is necessary. In over 20 years in professional workplaces, I have seen far more people terminated primarily because of bad attitudes rather than poor performance. Employers are people, and most people can work around performance issues much easier than they can work around issues of consistently poor attitudes. One reason for this is that a poor performer only has a direct impact on the work one person was responsible for, whereas a poor attitude affects everyone near that person, including co-workers, customers, and others. Before we explore these thorny issues, let us look at the most straightforward terminations.

Causes for Immediate (Or Near Immediate) Termination

- Theft—stealing
- Fraud—making false documents or statements for personal gain
- Endangering the safety of someone at work
- Drugs or alcohol use on the job
- Breaking the law
- Harassment—sexual, ethnic, religious, or otherwise

For all but some cases of harassment, the answer is immediate termination. The employee should be confronted right away. He or she should be taken into an office and told to leave work immediately and not come back. In situations that violate the law, you may be advised to call law enforcement. This is particularly true for theft. Document specifically what evidence exists and what actions you as the supervisor took. Put this information in writing and place it in the employee's personnel file.

Figure 13.1. Challenging personnel issues must be dealt with Do not ignore issues, or they will persist.

Harassment

Harassment may fall into the category for immediate termination if it is obvious, extreme, and witnessed by more than one person. If it was less than obvious, or only witnessed by one person, you might need further investigation and other, lesser disciplinary action. The reason for a broader range of actions for harassment is that a wide range of actions from subtle to extreme can be seen as harassment, and some people have higher and lower sensitivity to these issues. A case of a comment or action that is perceived as subtle harassment by some may be able to be corrected by talking to the offending employee about what types of comments, jokes or actions are appropriate in a work environment. The key is to match the action to the offense, and to not tolerate a pattern of behavior that makes employees feel targeted for harassment at work. Since harassment can be among the most litigious issues, as a supervisor it is important that any claim of harassment be dealt with immediately, and that all actions be documented, in case the problem persists.

Other employee behavior issues that need to be addressed by supervisors include the following:

- Appears bored, no commitment
- Will not follow up on issues
- Is insubordinate, will not follow direction
- Is argumentative
- Gossips
- Has anger management issues
- Displays bad attitude

Unlike the issues that merit immediate action, the list above, while less significant, can be more challenging to deal with because the behaviors are less severe. Often issues like these are ignored by supervisors, because they do not rise to the level that "must" be addressed. However, these issues can be very corrosive to a workplace, lowering the morale and productivity of those around the challenged employee.

Some of these issues might be able to be resolved by making it clear what the workplace expectations are and what behaviors are not acceptable. These issues might seem obvious to some but might not be universally understood. When it is simply a communication issue, a resolution can be easy. With some people, the drive for their inappropriate actions such as anger or insubordination may be deeply rooted in their personality and past experience, and it might not be possible to resolve the issues. Most supervisors would like to believe that they can reform an employee on the wrong path, but in truth motivation and a willingness to change behavior is internally rooted within a person. If the employee is committed to change, he/she might be able to, but this is not something that the supervisor can control.

What the supervisor can do is to communicate clearly what is expected and help those that want to improve. This approach takes time and effort from both the supervisor and the employee and involves the following steps:

- Make work expectations very clear.
- Set up meetings to discuss the issue; make the employee aware what you will be meeting about and that you are open to solutions.
- Start on a positive note and listen (it is always good to start with a compliment of some good behavior, then move to the challenging issue).
- Focus on behaviors (objective and specific).
- Confirm agreement on next steps.
- Focus on future actions.
- Record meeting notes and put in file.
- Follow up with a meeting in a few weeks.

Marginal Performance

While the causes for immediate termination are very clear cut, and the second group of issues including anger, gossip, and insubordination are more challenging, perhaps the most challenging issues are those of mediocre performers. These are employees who do not trigger any of the issues we have covered, which would be fairly obvious issues that need to be addressed. These are employees who simply do not perform their jobs at a very high level. They do their jobs, they just do not do a great job. In most workplaces, these people continue doing marginal work for years. Most supervisors do not know what to do with these employees to improve their performance. Some of the actions that can be taken to improve these marginal performers are listed here:

- Set a good example and publicly praise good performance, so the benchmark is understood by everyone.
- Hold supervisors accountable for either improving mediocre employees' performance or moving them out.
- Look for a different job within the organization that would match their aptitude.
- Give them clearly defined projects that they are responsible for (often C performers are sheltered too much). If they are not held accountable for specific results, it is difficult to document low performance.
  - See that they have all the tools for success.
  - Ask for a written action plan.
  - Make sure they know they will be held accountable for their performance.
  - Follow up.

Terminating Employment

When all the steps covered above have failed to resolve the performance issues, it is time to consider the last resort of termination.

Supervisors should be communicating with their boss as well as the person in charge of human resources/personnel at this stage. It is important to have a very clear knowledge of personnel law, policies, and other issues like a collective bargaining (union) agreement.

With any termination, the supervisor needs to consider the fired employee's due diligence. What process of appeal could they use if they feel the action is not justified? With the worst offenses that merit immediate termination, there is much less likelihood of appeal because the offense was of an obvious nature. With the less obvious performance issues, there is a greater chance of appeal. You do not want to terminate employment unless you and the human resources department both agree the case for firing is strong.

Documentation is the key to a strong case for termination. Multiple memos to the personnel file, with specifics about performance issues and steps taken to communicate the issues with the employee, and lessor efforts to resolve the issues. All of these memos should be dated, so it is clear that there has been an ongoing effort to resolve the issues. While such formal documentation is ideal, it can also be useful to have other less formal or dated notes detailing efforts to resolve any issues. The purpose of these notes and memos is to have a documented timeline of how the employee was communicated with about performance issues and the chances available to resolve them. This documentation should cover "just the facts." While it is natural to be frustrated and even angry as the supervisor of an employee who is not working to resolve issues, the more objective you can be, the stronger the case is for the termination.

The Meeting

The time has come; months of work to resolve the issues have failed. The personnel file has clear documentation that communications to the employee were clear and opportunities to correct performance have failed. You, as the supervisor, have communicated with both your boss and the human resources department what the next step is. Now it is time to bring the employee's employment with your organization to an end.

Key steps of the termination meeting

- Have a witness there (maybe HR or another manager of a higher rank than the terminated employee). This will help if the employee challenges the termination or claims you said inappropriate things.

- Be direct; reference the previous meetings, but do not rehash everything. Often the employee will be in denial about what is happening and will want to debate the previous actions. This is not the meeting to give another chance; once the decision has been made to end employment, it should be a very businesslike and factual end. Do not allow the meeting to drag out.

- Have the meeting in a place where it is not obvious to other employees. Personnel issues should be kept as private as possible. To respect the privacy of the terminated employee on a very difficult day, have the meeting behind closed doors, out of view from others, with the exception of your invited witness.

- Make this the person's final day on the job; do not keep the employee around. Once the person has been fired, there is no good that can come from him or her being around. The employee can lower the morale of others and could be a risk for some kind of sabotage. Supervise the clearing out of personal things so there is no time or opportunity to do damage.

- Do not apologize or reconsider the termination decision during the meeting. You can certainly say that you are sorry that things have come to this point. But remember that the employee has had numerous opportunities to correct performance issues, and the employee has failed to improve the situation. It should be a difficult decision to terminate anyone other than those who do engage in the activities that merit immediate termination, so when the decision has been made, follow through with it. Do not change your mind mid-meeting.

Termination, disciplinary actions, and meetings to talk about poor performance are all difficult and uncomfortable things to do for all parties involved. This is why too often challenging personnel issues are not dealt with and are ignored by supervisors. Sometimes poorly performing employees are transferred around as supervisors try to push them off on someone else. Delays, inaction, and passing the problem along never solves the issue. And while the issue with one employee is ongoing, it adversely affects the morale of all other employees around, as they witness the unresolved issues. To build an organization that is performance focused, you must expect and demand the best from everyone. Using the Viking analogy from earlier in the book, those who are not pulling on the oars while the others do will take the ship off course and slow your progress. Will others continue to give their best, when they see someone not performing and not being held accountable? In the end, organizations are not about facilities, programs, or equipment, they are about people. Only when the people of an organization are doing their jobs well and striving to do even better can it be a high performance organization.

While agencies have many kinds of assets and many approaches or tools for success, at the core, most organizations are really just a collection of people trying to achieve common goals. Because of this, human resources are the most important kind of resources any organization can have. You need people who are smart, motivated, and all working in the same direction. Most of this can be achieved by hiring the best, providing first-rate training, and fostering good supervisors who can coach and mentor those who report to them to achieve the best results. Because people have so many individual differences and because the various part of our personal and professional lives are so intertwined, managing people is one of the most challenging, and sometimes rewarding tasks in any organization.

Getting the people side of an agency "right" is critical to success. History is filled with great examples of small groups with limited resources that were able to achieve greatness because they were tight teams that were willing to work hard and smartly toward a common goal. When the right team is in place and working well together, job satisfaction and productivity are high, and anything is possible.

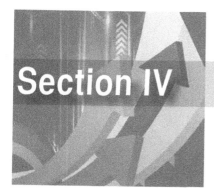

Section IV

Financial Resources

There are many potential measures of health for an organization. Does it have a clear sense of mission? Is the morale high among the employees? Is there a sense of forward momentum? While these measures are not financial, many of the most common measures of organizational success are.

To be a high performance agency, it is essential to have strong financial performance, or at least a plan to achieve health. Growth needs to be part of the goal, or as we have seen with organizational life cycle, when growth stops, the long process of stagnation and decline begins. A sense that the finances are strong and improving is a powerful tool to creating a sense of positive momentum and growing employee morale. So, regardless of how powerful financial motivation is within the culture of a given agency, it cannot be overlooked. When these factors are moving in the right direction, they can make great things possible, and when they are moving in the wrong direction, they will kill any sense of positive momentum.

Budgeting

Funding Organizational Priorities

"Don't tell me where your priorities are, show me where you spend your money, and I'll tell you what they are."

—James W. Frick

One route to distinguishing yourself as a top performer in any organization is to understand the organization's budget and participate in the annual budgeting process. Many people steer away from budgets because they do not see themselves as "numbers people." Budgets do not require complicated math and are much more about setting priorities than doing equations. So, takes some time and show some initiative to learn about your organization's budget. With this knowledge, volunteer to engage in the development of whatever part of your budget is appropriate.

In the "bad old days," budgets were just pages of numbers showing revenues and expenses, and while they still serve this most basic function of showing revenues and expenses, today a good budget serves many other roles, including the following:

- **Planning**
  - How is the next year going to be the same or different from the experience of last year?

- **Coordinating and communicating**
  - A budget should express some of the key priorities of the year, and what the fiscal environment is that the organization is experiencing

- **Monitoring progress**
  - In addition to dollars and cents, a budget should also express the goals and measurable results that the organization has.

- **Evaluating performance**
  - With the measurable results that the budget should have, the effectiveness of the programs related to those measurable results can be seen.

One of the great advantages of evolving a budget from purely financial issues to one that includes strategic programs and operational goals is that the budget becomes the central document of the organization. As long as it is purely financial, only a certain number of people will engage with it. If only the budget and finance people are looking at the budget, it cannot be an effective tool for organizational change and growth. When it becomes the central document where all major goals, financial and otherwise, are tracked, a much wider range of staff will engage with the document, and it will become a vital reference for many. When this happens, the budget can be an important tool to growing an organization in various ways.

Reading a Budget

In reading a budget page like the City of Boston example in Figure 14.1, there are two types of columns, "actual" and "budget."

CITY OF BOSTON
BUDGET SUMMARY
(Dollars in Millions)

REVENUES	FY09 Actual	FY10 Actual	FY11 Budget	FY12 Budget
Property Tax Levy	1,400.71	1,475.93	1,539.68	1,608.23
Overlay Reserve	(35.43)	(35.73)	(37.35)	(39.23)
Excises	106.85	103.42	105.35	132.93
Fines	70.40	70.67	70.41	68.58
Interest on Investments	17.84	3.18	2.00	2.00
Payments In Lieu of Taxes	33.95	34.94	35.70	39.48
Urban Redevelopment Chapter 121A	65.46	66.59	56.60	58.10
Misc. Department Revenue	71.57	64.48	133.14	54.23
Licenses and Permits	41.01	30.56	32.49	34.10
Penalties & Interest	7.78	7.96	7.71	7.76
Available Funds	14.19	17.08	17.11	17.07
State Aid	454.44	413.21	395.70	366.99
Teachers Pension Reimbursement	118.84	0.00	0.00	0.00
Total Recurring Revenue	2,367.60	2,252.29	2,358.53	2,350.22
Budgetary Fund Balance	35.00	45.00	45.00	35.00
Non-Recurring Revenue	0.00	5.98	6.00	1.00
Total Revenues	2,402.60	2,303.27	2,409.53	2,386.22

Figure 14.1. Sample budget

If you want to know how the organization has actually performed, the "actual" columns show what really happened in years past. This is the most important measure to consider in building a new budget, because it shows results as opposed to just intentions.

The "budget" column shows what the intended revenues and expenses were for fiscal years that have not been finished yet. Remember that fiscal years do not necessarily match calendar years, so understand when your fiscal year starts and ends. If your fiscal year starts on July 1, 2014 and ends June 30, 2015, that would be called fiscal year 2015, because you always name a fiscal year for the calendar year in which it ends.

Types of Budgets

Rolling 12-Month Budget

Organizations that use this type of budget plan for each month of the year and update their budget every month with one new month of projection being added each month, so they always have 12 months planned out. Some advantages of this type of budget include the following:

- It is highly flexible to changing circumstances since it is updated monthly rather than yearly.
- It always gives a 12-month projection, whereas an annual budget only does this in the first month of the fiscal year.
- The flexibility of this method is great for startup organizations without a track record of results or for an organization undergoing big changes in how it operates.

The fundamental weakness of this methodology is that it is continually ongoing. Most organizations have a budget season where they develop the budget for the coming year, and then they can move on to focus on implementing it. Organizations using the 12-month rolling budget live in budget season all the time, which takes time and energy away from other important priorities. An organization with this type of budget will have a fiscal year set for reporting on its annual performance (filing tax returns if needed), but since updating the budget is a monthly or ongoing process, the fiscal year loses some of the importance it has in other organizations where the budget is tied to a certain 12-month time period.

Incremental Budget

Most organizations have some form of incremental budget. At one level, this means that you base your current budget on the budgets and performance of previous years. How it is implemented depends on the organization. In its best application, an organization leaves alone the part of the budget and operations that are performing well and focuses on certain areas of either great challenge or great opportunity. By being incremental (or based on past performance), you do not need to "reinvent the wheel," but can focus efforts on where they will have the greatest impact.

The worst way an incremental budget can be implemented is to base it solely on past performance and not use the budget as a tool for change. One large park system develops its annual budget by looking at the actual performance from the last completed year. It then takes all the revenue lines and increases them by 3%, and all the expense lines and increases them by 3%. That is it.

This is a budget approach without any thought, insight, or effort to change. The assumption that all revenues will go up by a standard 3% is disconnected from any market insight. In reality, there is probably have some revenue that can go up much more, and some that is flat or declining. Assuming that all expenses will go up by 3% is equally negligent. Some expenses are likely going up much faster, and others could go down if efforts were focused in those areas. This agency also develops its budget with a small group of people at headquarters without any significant input from facility managers who will need to implement the budget. The other problem with this approach is if everyone knows that next year's budget will be based mostly on the actual results from two years before, with 3% added per year, there is no incentive to perform better than budgeted because you are expected to keep revenues up and expenses down in the future. For years, federal budgets have had this problem, where if they underspent in one year, they would automatically get less in the future.

Systems drive behavior, and it is easy to see that the budget that is not modified based on opportunities and challenges, but is purely derived from past performance in a solely incremental way, will drive an organization into mediocrity. You cannot have a high performing organization and a brain-dead budgeting process. The budget needs to be a tool for change and growth.

In summary, there are two kinds of incremental budgets. One uses the ability not to change everything too fast to focus change efforts in targeted areas and get results. The other disconnects the budget from market realities so it is not a meaningful or central document in the organization.

Zero-Based Budget

The most radical of budget approaches is the zero-based budget. Despite having years of past budgets and actuals, this approach ignores all past performance and attempts to reinvent every line item of the budget from scratch. Forget how things have been done. In a perfect world, how would you approach that function of the organization; what revenues could you generate? And what expenses do you think you will need? This approach is generally used only for a year or two during a period of radical reinvention. "Question everything," could be the motto of this approach.

An advantage to this approach is that it sends a clear message through-out the organization that you are in a new time, and the practices of the past need to be justified or thrown out. If an organization needs a rapid turnaround, using a zero-based budget can be a tool for getting this done.

The disadvantages of this approach are twofold: one, this is a very dis-ruptive approach, where even elements of the operations that are perform-ing well are upended; and two, without relying on past performance, it is almost inevitable that some significant elements of the budget will be overlooked, and some expenses or revenues not anticipated, creating fur-ther disruption. While this model can help bring about big changes, it is unlikely that many organizations can sustain this approach for many years without the process becoming so counterproductive that it needs to be traded for another method.

Role of Various Parties in the Budget Process

From the president and congress to a community nonprofit and every organization in between, the basic elements of the budget process are the same. The CEO (president, executive director, city manager, etc.) prepares a proposed budget and submits it to the governance board (congress, city council, board of directors), and the board ultimately adopts the budget, sometimes with modifications. Let's examine how this process works at different levels.

Mid-Level Staff

Generally, lower level staff do not have a lot of input in the budget. But a high performance organization will engage the staff that is respon-sible for the operation of different units of the agency. Maybe that is the

As a central document in any agency, the creation of the budget can offer *great leadership opportunities* at many levels in an organization.

manager or assistant manager of a facility or someone in charge of some other area of programs or operations. These people should be engaged in the development of the proposed budget that the CEO will ultimately propose, because they will be responsible for implementing the budget once it is adopted.

From a management perspective, promising employees that you see as moving into higher management in the future should be invited to be a part of budget meetings, so they can start to see how the organization works and what their future roles might be like. This is a way of growing the talent you will need to manage the organization in the future.

From the perspective of an employee who would like to move up in the organization, you should look for opportunities to be a part of the budget process, because it will demonstrate your understanding of the big picture and show your initiative. One way of doing this would be to understand the budget development calendar and, before it is due, volunteer to do some market research on the competition and come up with some revenue and expense projections for next year on some part of the operation that you know. If you make this offer to someone who needs to create a bigger part of the budget, he or she is likely to be grateful for your help. This makes your boss look good, and you look good in the process.

Senior Staff

While the CEO officially submits the proposed budget and must buy off on the proposal, the whole senior staff is generally busy pulling together their pieces of the whole budget. A big part of being in the senior staff team is having a hand in the development of the proposed budget. At this level, it is important to be attuned to the political and strategic priorities of the organization. To be successful, the budget must first meet the approval of the CEO who will sign off on it, and the governance board that will provide the ultimate adoption. Because of this, one of the key roles for the senior staff team is to take the interests and desires of the staff in the field and mesh those as well as can be done with the macro priorities of the governance board and CEO.

CEO and Governance Board

The official process that exists in most organizations is that the person in the CEO position (city manager, nonprofit president, executive director) submits the draft budget in a complete form to the governance board (county council, board of directors, etc.) which has the role of adopting the final budget. Since the budget is the vehicle for setting and funding organizational priorities, it is the role of both the CEO and board to make sure that the budget is in alignment with the policy, political, and strategic priorities of the organization. If the CEO does a good job, there should be little change between what he or she proposes and what is adopted by the governance board. If the CEO is not in step with the board, there might be several reasons. First, perhaps the board is not in agreement with itself. Perhaps there are factions on the board that are in conflict with each other. In this case, it will be difficult for the CEO to propose a budget that everyone likes. This is often seen in boards divided with partisan/political strife. Second, the CEO and board may be in conflict with each other, with different visions of where the organization should be going. One of the best ways to avoid this dynamic is to have a good strategic plan that has been formally adopted, and then it is up to the CEO to propose a budget that advances the plan and to communicate to the board how the budget does this. Good communication between the board and the CEO can head off disagreements over the budget.

Sometimes, board members will have insights that the CEO or senior management did not see and will help shape the budget to address these important issues. Sometimes, they may make budget changes for political consumption. Sometimes, changes can be driven by pet issues. One board member may have expertise in an area and feel he or she can or should adjust those line items that address that niche. In the end, the adoption of the budget is the action of the whole governance board and should reflect an agreement between management and governance on the priorities of the year.

Sections of a Budget

Budgets are not universal in their structure, but top-quality budgets have some commonalities. In general terms, they should communicate the goals and objectives of the organization. They should explain to the reader what the organization does. They should connect the strategic goals of the organization with the funding priorities of the agency. To do these things well, a good budget really needs more than just spreadsheets of revenues and expenses. Those spreadsheets are always going to be the foundation, but if they are all there is, your budget is unlikely to become the vehicle for organizational change and development that it can be. The following are some additional sections that are important.

Budget Message

This letter from the CEO to the reader should highlight the most important issues and set the tone for the whole budget. If you read this one letter, you should have a very good picture of the main issues facing the organization.

Budget-in-Brief or Summary

This section should be graphically rich with many charts and graphs that highlight the significant issues. Charts are one of the most powerful tools used in communicating finances. As with most financial factors, the "amount" of revenues or expenses for a given year are not as important as the trend. What directions are the numbers going? How is the market changing? If you want to see trends of the significant elements of finances, you need charts that describe what has been happening in the market over a number of years.

General Fund

In public sector budgets, the general fund is the portion that covers operations funded with tax dollars. Often this includes general administration and elements of the operations that do not generate significant funds. The general fund tends to have one main revenue line, which is the tax funding, and maybe a few others related to grants and interest income.

Enterprise Fund

The essence of an enterprise fund is that it is similar to running a business within a larger government budget. One of the great advantages is that while general fund revenues may get redeployed at the end of a year to other governmental needs, year-end revenues that generally stay in the enterprise fund are carried forward into the next year. This creates something like a "profit motive" with a government. Unlike a private-sector profit, the owners cannot take the money out, but like a business, the profits (often called "net revenue") can be reinvested.

High performance parks, recreation, and tourism organizations should take advantage of the benefits of enterprise funds to encourage an entrepreneurial spirit in the organization.

The private sector does not have the general fund/enterprise fund divide in that their entire budget is one big enterprise fund.

Cost Centers

Specific operations should be broken down in the budget to the level that will be of greatest use for management. This means in some facilities/parks, it can be presented as one cost center if the areas of enterprise are not too great. If one facility has multiple operations that are sizable, it may be good to break each out as a different cost center. The end purpose of the budget is as a management tool, and if too much is rolled up into one cost center, it may "hide" management issues that would be seen if it were broken out.

Within the cost center, there should also be site-specific measurable results such as number of participants, programs, events, goals for the facility for the coming year, and information on whether the goals from last year were met. If facilities' budgets have goals and those goals connect to the organizational goals, then you have a powerful tool for organizational change. If it is just revenues and expenses for the upcoming year, you might fail to answer the all-important "why" questions. Why are we engaged in this enterprise, and what do we plan to accomplish?

Cost centers live within the enterprise or general funds, based on what the function of the cost center is.

Capital Budget

In addition to the operating budget that covers the planned expenses for operating the facility for the year (combination of general and enterprise funds), the capital budget covers major investments in land, facilities, and equipment. These are items over a certain value ($10,000+, $25,000+) and with a long-term life (often 10+ years). Specific definitions of capital assets vary somewhat in different organizations, but the basics are the same. They are long-term assets that are more than an annual expense. Some capital assets, such as equipment and most buildings, depreciate over time (lose some percentage of their value and their useful life is consumed), and some assets, such as land, appreciate in value over time.

Within governments, capital assets can be purchased with general revenues or often with bond funds. A bond is a loan that a government takes from financial institutions. These bonds usually are given at significantly better rates than commercial loans.

Types of Bonds

General obligation bonds are the most common kind of funding for government capital development. These bonds are paid for with general revenue tax dollars. The rates on this type of financing are usually the best, because the loaner views the tax base of a city, county, or state as a good financial risk, so long as they have not borrowed too much already. Most governments make it a high priority to keep a high bond rating. In the world of bond ratings, AAA is considered the best, followed by AA, A, AB, B, and so on. If a government borrows or spends more than its tax base can support, its rating is reduced, and that results in higher interest rates, which drive up the cost of capital projects.

In many cases, the citizens of an area will need to vote on and pass a levy (tax) to support a specific set of projects. So there needs to be good public support of bond initiatives or they can be voted down.

Revenue bonds are another kind of public financing that is much closer to a business loan. For this kind of financing, the loan is paid for by the revenues that the project will generate. It only works for projects with a reasonably strong net revenue (profit) that can support the bond payments in addition to the operating costs of the facility that is built.

Land Acquisition

Create a Legacy of Growth

In nature, organisms are either in the process of growing or in the process of dying. Agencies and organizations are much the same, as we learned in looking at organizational life cycles; when an organization stops the growth phase, it has a high likelihood of slipping into decline. Often that decline is not even seen by many in the organization until it is advanced. One of the best ways to avoid this is to continue to focus on growth. Grow lands, facilities, programs, or some other important aspect of your mission. The important thing is to be on a growth footing, looking for and acting on opportunities.

The most central mission of any parks or recreation agency is to create public open space. So whenever new lands are being acquired, you are engaged in the most important part of your mission. It is easy for the focus

Most central to the mission of any park agency

is to creat public open space.

to turn to existing operations to the exclusion of growth, but this is a grave mistake.

While there are many approaches and skills involved in land acquisition, the most critical tool is the simplest. It is to be open to opportunities! When you are not open to and looking for opportunities, you will not find them, and when you are, they will often find you. The next most important consideration is to make land acquisition a priority. If it is a priority, you will include funds in your budget and you will actively seek additional funds to augment your efforts.

Agencies that prioritize land acquisition are usually very successful in their efforts. Columbus and Franklin County Metro Parks (Ohio) averages almost 1,000 acres of new park land per year because it recognizes the importance of parks and trails to the long-term success, health, and attractiveness of the community.

Land Selection

Because it is usually expensive, the decision to buy land needs to be done in a thoughtful manner. And to do this, it is critical to have a clear idea of what type of lands your organization would like to add. One of the best ways to be able to consider many different properties and keep the focus on what the desired characteristics are is to have a point-based land selection criteria. This scoring system allows you to identify all the potentially desirable attributes and place a value on each one. Some of these might work in opposite directions, such as the ability to build new facilities, which would mean more expensive and less ecological land might be the opposite of the desire to conserve a rare habitat. If these are both desires, that is great, and they can both be scored on the selection criteria, but the same land will have very different scores in these two categories.

Developing the land selection criteria should be a process that the governance board is involved with, and one in which it should vote on the criteria since it will impact how different properties are scored.

With a developed criteria, any potential land acquisition (or donation) can be evaluated and graded, and this then will help the governance board determine if it should be pursued and how much, if any, should be offered as a purchase price. Some properties might be "must haves," others are "ought to haves," while some would be "nice to have." Determination whether the price is right will vary depending on how important it is to your community. The selection criteria help make the determination of which is which.

Take this a step further and develop a land acquisition strategy that identifies the properties that the park system is most interested in acquiring. Having a written document can help keep the priorities in front of the park board. In some states, a strategy like this is privileged information, but in others it might be a public document that requires care in how you present the information. You don't want to start off on the wrong foot with a landowner who learns about your interest in the media.

Even with developed criteria, you must remain open to opportunities. Great opportunities that help to protect important natural areas or provide new park facilities can arise that you didn't anticipate in your criteria. For example, in Columbus, Ohio, the Metro Parks system contributed to a dam removal project that created 32 acres of new downtown parkland that was previously underwater. The project, which also improved water quality, was funded primarily by businesses and other levels of government. A small contribution to the project yielded large dividends.

Finding Land

Sometimes, people with land to sell will approach an agency, and the agency can decide whether to pursue the deal or not. Other times, you might need to seek out the properties that fit your criteria. One route is to hire a realtor. The advantage is that the realtor will have access to the listings of all the properties that are for sale. The disadvantage is that there is a commission to be paid to the realtor, and almost all realtors really work for the seller. The one exception to this is if you specifically hire a "buyer's agent."

The other disadvantage to using a realtor and considering currently listed properties is that you are dealing with sellers who already have a price in mind and are interested in selling to the highest bidder. Realtors working on a percentage of the purchase price want to see every property sold for as much as possible. This is not where you will find great deals.

A preferable alternative to the realtor model is to seek out lands through direct contact with the landowners. If you know what you are looking for, you can use maps and property records to determine who owns lands that your agency might like to buy. Contact these landowners directly and see if any of them would like to see their land become a park. Only some will be interested in doing a deal, but one of those might actually be a great deal. Some of the other landowners will know that you are interested and will hopefully contact you first when they decide it is time to sell. This often yields productive results.

Landowners attracted to the legacy of helping to make a new park might donate all or a portion of their land to the cause. If no realtors are involved, then you do not need to pay for their commissions. With a willing owner and a willing seller, an attorney can create the deed and other documents to complete the transaction.

Fee Simple Acquisition

The most straightforward type of acquisition is to just buy the property. A willing seller and a willing buyer agree on a price, and the deal is done. It sounds easy, and sometimes it is. Some of the considerations in a simple purchase are the following:

- **Appraisal.** A professional appraisal can assure everyone that a fair value is being paid. If grants are a part of the acquisition funding, it is highly likely that an appraisal will be necessary.
- **Survey.** Often tax records can be inaccurate regarding the size of properties, and a survey provides an accurate account of the exact size and boundaries of the property. A modified ALTA survey is usually the best approach since it provides much more information than a boundary only survey.
- **Title insurance.** This assures that you have a legitimate title for the property you are buying and is generally considered a must for acquisitions.

Land Donations

It is very common for individuals to donate land for parks and open space. These people love the land and want to leave a legacy of public open space for future generations to enjoy. It is a very noble cause. Sometimes there is a prolonged "courtship" period, where potential land donors determine if they want to give the land and if they want to give it to your organization. In this way, these land donations are not free from the perspective of time and energy but can be extremely well worth it.

Land that is donated, either entirely or some portion of its value, is a charitable contribution with tax benefits. It counts as a tax deduction on a federal level, and states give such donations either deduction status or in some cases tax credit status. In several states, the tax credits can be quite generous.

The longer landowners have owned the property, the more likely they are to be concerned about their legacy and the greater their capital gains are likely to be if they sell for full value. They can offset some or all of their capital gains through a donation or bargain sale.

Bargain Sale

The difference between buying land and having it donated is not all or nothing. A landowner can choose to sell a property for less than its appraised value to a qualified organization, and the difference between what is paid for it and what it is worth is a charitable donation. This option is great for people who want to see their land become a park but need some amount of money for it.

Land Trusts and Other Partners

A land trust is a certain class of nonprofit organization that is set up primarily for the preservation/conservation of property. The best known trusts are the large national ones such as the Nature Conservancy, Conservation Fund, and Trust for Public Land, but there are around 1,400 land trusts in the U.S. Many of these are very small, all-volunteer groups. So the organizational capacity of different land trusts can be radically different, but because they are all about land conservation (or sometimes historic preservation), they can be valuable allies in the task of acquiring new parkland.

One way they can help is that they might be aware of who is interested in donating all or part of the value of their land, because that is the business they are involved in. Most conservation organizations have a higher interest in seeing the land preserved than in managing the property after it is preserved, and this is where a park agency can be a good partner for a land trust. One example of this dynamic is the Civil War Trust, a national organization with great abilities to raise private funds, get federal and state grants, and target significant Civil War sites for conservation. While they manage some sites, their primary mission is conservation, so they are great partners for park systems who can manage the sites, interpret the history, and make them open and accessible to the public. It is a win-win deal when two organizations can combine their complementary expertise to achieve their collective missions.

Other nonprofits or governmental organizations can also make great partners if the missions and priorities align. Too often, people and organizations limit themselves by only thinking of their own internal resources. Through partnerships, your internal resources or lack of them need not be a limiting factor. Just as the first rule of land acquisition was to be open to possibilities, the same holds true for partnerships. Be open to working with others, and exciting new possibilities will make themselves known. Ninety percent of success in this area is to be open to possibilities.

State and federal agencies can often be great partners. There are many grant programs that can provide funding to assist with a purchase. In some areas, legislators are supportive of park agencies through capital appropriations. These government agencies usually require accountability, which some people see as strings being attached. But if your missions are aligned, then this can be a great source of funding.

Conservation Easements

The primary tool for most land trusts is the conservation easement. This tool has been effectively used to preserve millions of acres of land.

Land ownership is like a bundle of sticks; some sticks allow the owner to live on the land, some allow it to be developed to the full extent that local zoning permits, and some allow for agriculture or mining rights. All the sticks together are what we think of as land ownership. But with a conservation or preservation easement, the owner can give or sell a "partial interest" or partial ownership in the land to another party. How this is used by land trusts is that they enable land owners who want to see their property preserved forever to give the trust just those rights that would otherwise allow the landowner to develop the property. While it is generally a donation of these partial interests, in effect it is extinguishing or eliminating these development rights, and usually for forever. What the landowner gets, in addition to the knowledge that the land will never be fully developed (even by future owners), is a tax benefit from the donation. An appraiser will provide a value for what the land would be worth with all the development rights intact, and another for what the land is worth with the easement restrictions. The difference is the value of the donation. This value is a state and federal tax deduction, just as if the owner had donated that much cash to a charitable organization. Some states also have a tax credit for that donation, which makes it even more valuable.

To be eligible for these tax benefits, easements need to meet certain IRS defined standards, one of which is that the easement is permanent and designed to preserve certain environmental, recreational (such as trails) or historic features of the property that are called "conservation values." Besides being permanent, conserving conservation values, and being donated to a conservation organization such as a land trust or park agency, each conservation easement is customized to the land and the desires of the landowner. The more development value they give up, the higher the tax benefits of the easement, but that varies. Some landowners will reserve some development rights and some will extinguish them all.

The reason easements are important to the acquisition of parks, and potential tourism sites is that they are a tool to lower the acquisition costs. In many cases, an agency will not need all the development rights of a property to fit its goals for a new park. But without an easement, the cost will likely reflect the full development potential. Buying land that already has an easement on it, or working with the landowners to place an easement on the property prior to the purchase, can be a strategy for cost-effective land acquisition.

One potential downside to easements is that future landowners might not understand, accept, or appreciate the restrictions imposed on the property by the conservation easement. This can lead to conflicts with those landowners whose property is encumbered by the easement.

Maintaining a focus on growth is critical for any organization. With park agencies, the most important kind of growth is the physical growth of the public lands. Creating public lands is at the core of why there are parks and park agencies, and engaging in land acquisitions, large or small, is central to living up to the mission. Mature agencies and ones in urbanized areas might think that their land acquisition days are behind them. But this type of thinking is self-fulfilling. Resist such beliefs and keep looking for growth opportunities. Make land acquisition a priority and seize opportunities!

Governance

Financial Oversight and Policy Direction

Every legally formed organization, company, government, or nonprofit has a governance function, and yet many people are not clear on what this role is all about.

Governance usually comes from an elected or appointed board. Such boards go by different names, and depending on what type of organization they are connected with, they include board of directors, city or county council, congress, and other variations of these. In most organization charts, they are at the top of the pyramid, with the CEO position reporting to them and the rest of the organization reporting to the CEO.

One of the key reasons governance boards are required for most organizations is to provide checks and balances. The board is in charge of hiring and firing the CEO and responsible for financial oversight of the organization. This does not mean that they do the accounting for the organization, but it does mean that the auditors who review the books and make an independent assessment are hired by the board and report to the board. It also means that a governance board has the responsibility to keep an eye on the finances of the organization.

With a number of major failures of the financial oversight function of corporate boards in the early 2000s, Congress enacted the Sarbanes-Oxley legislation, which held directors of publicly traded companies much more responsible for financial oversight.

The second big area of responsibility of a governance board is that of policy direction. This means that the board is directly engaged in formulating and adopting the policy positions of the organization. This includes the strategic plan of the agency.

This role with the strategic plan is the second most important function of the board next to the financial oversight. As a result, any board/organization that does not have an adopted strategic plan should have one, since that is the primary tool that boards have to guide the overall direction of the organization. It is not a board's job to manage an organization, or even get involved in how day-to-day operations take place, but it is the board's job to help set broad directional goals through the strategic plan.

One of the great challenges for any governance board is that they tend to be made up of high achieving doers, and yet their job is not a doing, hands-on role. This can be very difficult, especially when board members feel they have expertise in operational areas. The governance role feels very unnatural for many people, yet doing it well is critical to the overall success of the organization.

Related to the staff and operations of the organization, the board's one and only employee is generally the CEO (president, executive director, etc.). The board directly hires this CEO position, and that is the one employee they review, supervise, and can ultimately fire. Outside of this one

For the public to believe in the good works of your agency, they must trust that there is good governance, *and that begins with financial transparency.*

position, board members should not give directions to any other employee, regardless of how large or small the agency is. As a result, being a board member and interacting with the staff of an organization is challenging. Often, staff is unsure of the roles and authority of board members, and since many board members might be used to leading staff in other roles they have had in their lives, they need to be particularly careful in what they say and how they say it, so that they are not perceived as giving orders. The staff within any organization has some system of supervision and lines of authority, usually reflected on the organizational chart, and board members are largely outside of those lines of authority, except in how the board as a whole directs and reviews the CEO of the organization.

Because of the strange combination of the high level of responsibilities and significant limits of board members' authority, it can be challenging for people to understand and challenging to get the right balance of engagement in the right areas.

Peripheral Vision

As leaders in the community who are very familiar with the agency but not engaged in the day-to-day operations, one of the great roles a board can play is to help with the peripheral vision of the organization. What are the issues and trends that may be coming around the corner that the organization should be preparing for? Often, being too close to the current challenges can blind one to the future challenges, but the board can be in the perfect place to help address the future trends if they are looking for them. Like with all things, you only see  what you are looking for, so it is important for a board to be aware that this is one of their potential areas of contribution, so they can be thinking about trends that may be coming.

This theory of how organizations need to keep an eye on evolving trends that can have dramatic impacts on industries, was defined in the book *Peripheral Vision* by George S. Day and Paul J. H. Schoemaker, who are both professors at the Wharton School of Business. *Peripheral Vision* was published by Harvard Business School Press in 2006.

Newspapers have been made nearly obsolete by online news media. The once-mighty Kodak film and camera company is no longer around because of digital photography that made film processing unnecessary. Each of these industries did not see the change coming that ended their business model. They were big, strong industries with long track records that thought they would go on forever. Yet, each was brought down by a force they did not focus on soon enough.

So, what factors—political, technological, or societal—are out there as smaller issues today that have the potential to grow and threaten the foundation of your business model? To determine this, it is important to understand what your business model is. Every successful organization has one, or it would not exist. The business model of a city parks and recreation department might be something like:

> ## Potential City Park Agency Business Model
>
> - City has state authorization to collect property and sale taxes
> - City has an industrial and residential tax base that is adequate to support city government
> - City residents value park and recreation services provided by the city
> - City park agency generates 30% of operating revenues through service fees

This is a common business model that many local governments have. When it is defined as such, it is easy to see what kind of issues that are currently minor (peripheral) could challenge the model if they became major. Challenges to the status quo always seem far-fetched in the early stages.

The mighty British Empire did not consider it any significant issue when some rowdy people in Boston were killed by soldiers in 1770. But that small-scale issue in one Colonial city resulted in the founding of the United State of America a few years later.

The kinds of issues that could affect the business model of a city parks and recreation department would be issues that

- reduced the city's taxing authority,
- reduced the city's tax base,
- reduced the citizens' perceived value in city offered parks and recreation services, and
- reduced the agency's ability to generate 30% of its operating budget.

A wide range of issues that do not seem like big deals today could grow to challenge any one of a combination of these business model elements. As well connected community leaders, board members should be thinking about what elements could pose a threat one day and monitor those events, and, if necessary, advise the agency on how it might need to adapt to a new and changing environment. Staff that is engaged in the day-to-day operations might also see these issues, but because of their focus, it might be harder for them to see such side issues.

Meetings and Agendas

Since many people are more comfortable with details and operations than they are with the oversight and policy role of governance, the frequency and agendas of meetings are important. If a governance board meets too often, there simply will not be enough real governance issues to deal with, and they will slip deeper and deeper into nongovernance areas. Corporate boards tend to meet three to four times a year, and this can keep the meetings focused and targeted on big-picture governance issues. Some organizations have board meetings several times a month, and it is very hard to keep the focus where it should be with such frequent meetings. It is easier for organizations to have a great governance focus with an every-other-month meeting schedule. The less frequent schedule helps the board chair and CEO formulate a meeting agenda that is focused on significant issues and not filled with fluff. Better, more focused meetings both help the organization and the board members feel better about their important roles.

Other factors, such as the time of the day for meetings can have a big impact. If the meetings are in the morning, many people will want to see them accomplished in a manner that does not waste time, because some will need to move on to their jobs. Evening meetings can potentially drag on forever if they are not run well, as there is no external time limit like there is for a morning meeting.

Board retreats can be highly effective opportunities to deal with big issues that are not easily dealt with in a normal meeting. A retreat is often held in a location that is not the regular meeting place. A change of scenery can help people think about issues in new and different ways. Most retreats are also longer than a normal meeting, either all day or maybe two to three days. The longer format allows time to dig into a deep issue, and it also provides opportunities for board members to share meals and other time for social interaction. These opportunities can help the dynamics during the business meetings. An annual board retreat can be very useful in keeping a board engaged in large, governance-related issues and building the camaraderie that can help a board function well the rest of the year.

A highly effective tool for staying focused on the important big-picture issues is to have a well-articulated strategic plan. Such a plan should be focused on the "game-changing" steps that will lead the organization to achieve its mission. A plan that outlines the important strategic steps the organization wants to take can help a board chair and CEO focus meeting agendas around the agreed strategic issues.

Advisory Board and Friends Groups

Governance is a very specific role in organizations, and not every group that is called a board is a governance board. Many parks and recreation organizations have advisory boards that are made up of community leaders who are either appointed or self-selected to assist the agency. Such boards can raise funds, be a source of volunteer help, and assist with the peripheral vision needs of any organization. However, advisory boards do not have the powers of a governance board. They do not allocate funding through the budget, and the CEO (director, president) does not work for them. They are there to help but not to set the direction or see that it is implemented. Such advisory groups can be extremely valuable in connecting the agency with the community groups that are served. They help build political support for the agency and they can be a valuable sounding board for new ideas.

Friends groups are a type of advisory board. Often they have a function to raise money for a specific facility or set of facilities. Friends groups and advisory boards are a great way to channel the desire of people to help and volunteer and give them a higher sense of purpose beyond just individually volunteering their time and effort.

It is important for board members to have a very clear understanding of whether they are a governance or advisory board and what their powers and responsibilities are.

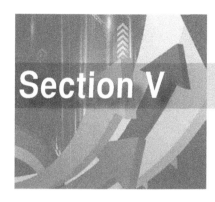

Section V

Creating a Brighter Future

In the previous chapters, the key skills and competencies of running a high performance organization have been covered. If these approaches have been well implemented, an organization should be performing well. The question now is how do you take a well-run agency in the field of parks, recreation, or tourism and change the world? That may sound grandiose, but it is very possible. Such organizations, when run well and growing, can enhance the lives of countless people in the communities they serve. And this impact makes the world (or at least a piece of it) a better place for everyone.

The following section covers the elements that take a good, high performing agency and help it reach its full potential to have a positive and transformational role in its community.

Positioning

What Is Your Value Proposition?

"Strategy is based on a differentiated customer value proposition. Satisfying [your] customers is the source of sustainable value creation."

—Robert Norton and David Kaplan
(Creators of the Balanced Scorecard)

Value Proposition

Every product and organization has its own value proposition. This idea of value proposition is the "deal" that is offered by the organization or product to the customer. Whether it is clearly stated or understood or not, there exists a "deal" or promise between the organization and the customer. Most organizations do not have a clear picture of what this deal is, but it exists, and understanding it is fundamental to building a strong organization.

> Value is a perception. When you position your agency as important to your community, *your agency is of higher value.*

The elements of the value proposition include the following:

- **Audience:** Who are your customers, whom do you serve?
- **Purpose:** What do you do?
- **Significance:** Is what you do important?
- **Uniqueness:** Is what you offer substantially different from what others offer?

If you can answer these questions for your organization, then you know the value proposition you are offering. If you do not know the answer to these questions, you should give this some thought, so you can articulate these issues.

Elevator Speech

Imagine a legislative body (federal, state, or local) is considering a bill that will directly affect your organization in an important way (either positive or negative). You find yourself in the elevator with one of the legislators who is about to vote on this bill and she asks, "So what do you do?" Being able to communicate who you serve, how you do it, and why it is important and unique in a clear and effective way, might make all the difference in how legislators vote on important bills.

Is Your Organization a Necessity or a Luxury?

Everyone would like to think that their work is necessary and important, and yet many parks and recreation agencies continue to brand themselves as "the fun agency." Fun is nice, but fun is not important and central to society. Many organizations in the public parks and recreation field still

Making Trails Transportation

*An Example of Positioning Parks as Important
to the Transportation System*

Trails have always helped people get around. But for 20th Century, and the first part of the 21st Century, many viewed trails as a nice recreational amenity and not a critical transportation system. The value that our society places on transportation can been seen in the $172 billion annual investment from all levels of govern-ment, according to the National Infrastructure Financing Commission (2012).

A great example of repositioning trails as a higher value asset can be seen in the San Francisco Bay Area, where the East Bay Regional Park District (EBRPD) received the largest federal grant for trails with $10.2 million awarded in 2010.

EBRPD was successful by selling their multi-county 175-mile paved trail system as a critical part of the region's transportation system. In doing this, the Federal Department of Transportation agreed to give them over $10 million to make connections and create a more integrated system.

At the time of the award, Doug Siden, the president of EBRPD's board said, "The park district has always been innovative in providing East Bay residents with opportunities that mesh well with their lifestyles, whether for work or recreating. This project, supported so well by our congressional delegation and area stakeholders, is very forward thinking about how to achieve healthy, livable, and sustainable communities that value walking, biking, and transit."

The winning grant proposal focused a great deal on connecting the existing trail network to existing bus and light rail transit stops. This approach essentially changed the product being sold from a traditional trail system to a higher value transportation system.

By repositioning the trail system, and looking to transportation funding sources vs. traditional parks and recreation funding sources, this ambitious project has become a national model.

> This large project is only partially funded by the big grant from DOT. In addition, EBRPD is now partnering with many other transportation-focused organizations, including the Metropolitan Transportation Commission, Alameda County Transportation Improvement Authority, Contra Costa Transportation Authority, West Contra Costa Transportation Advisory Committee, the San Francisco Bay Trail Project, and the cities of Dublin, Pleasanton, and Hercules.
>
> This example shows the power of both creating a large and compelling vision for the future, as well as positioning the assets and programs for the park agency in a way that give it a higher value to society and new set of partners moving forward.

use the term *leisure* in their titles. Few words convey insignificance more than the term *leisure*. The term had a more significant meaning decades ago, but today it means laying on the couch watching TV to many people. Even the term *recreation* is not as strong and important as one would like.

A good defining word includes *parks*. Everyone knows what a park is and that it is a valuable asset to the community. Terms such as *community enhancement, cultural, environmental, tourism,* and *destination* are all terms that denote value. Define yourself as important, and you have taken the first step to being important.

Below are links to great research funded by the National Recreation and Park Association that defines some of the major benefits of parks and recreation. Each of these links is to a significant research paper by a leading academic on the unique value that parks and recreation offer to the community. The values highlighted are not the typical ones that are used by most, which is why these are so valuable. When you deliver a predictable message, most people will not really listen. However if your message is outside the box, it is more likely to be noticed.

Measuring Economic Impact of Parks and Recreation Services
http://www.nrpa.org/uploadedFiles/nrpa.org/Publications_and_Research/Research/Papers/Crompton-Summary.PDF

- Sports tournaments, festivals, parks, and major recreation facilities operated by parks and recreation departments drive much of our tourism industry. Understand this connection between destinations and economic benefit to the community.

Parks Build Healthy Communities: Success Stories

http://www.nrpa.org/uploadedFiles/nrpaorg/Grants_and_Partners/ Recreation_and_Health/Resources/Case_Studies/Healthy-Communities-Success-Stories.pdf

- This article looks at healthy food, alternative transportation, and areas to recreate and how these factors connect to make places healthy or unhealthy to live.

Parks and Recreation in Underserved Areas: A Public Health Perspective

http://www.nrpa.org/uploadedFiles/nrpa.org/Publications_and_Research/Research/Papers/Parks-Rec-Underserved-Areas.pdf

- In addressing obesity and the health issues that go with this, we need to address access to parks and recreation facilities in underserved communities.

Parks and Recreation: Essential Partners in Active Transportation

http://www.nrpa.org/uploadedFiles/nrpa.org/Publications_and_Research/Research/ActiveTransportation_Final.HIGH.pdf

- This paper discusses the role of trails in creating a system of alternative transportation that results in both cleaner air and healthier people.

Rejuvenating Neighborhoods and Communities through Parks— A Guide To Success

http://www.nrpa.org/uploadedFiles/nrpa.org/Publications_and_Research/Research/Papers/Rejuvenating-Neighborhoods-White-Paper.pdf

- Using park development as means of community revitalization and economic development is covered in this paper.

Tourism is an enormous industry that generates a lot of state and local tax revenue. And tourism depends completely on interesting attractions to draw people to an area. This is one area where historic sites that are generally not considered economic assets can have a great positive effect on a community's economic vitality.

Below is a link to a report done by the Civil War Trust on the economic impact of historic tourism. This report is called Blue, Gray and Green: http://www.civilwar.org/land-preservation/blue-gray-and-green.pdf

In addition to a report like this, local destination marketing organizations (DMOs), sometimes known as convention and visitors bureaus, are great partners because they are also interested in promoting the tourism economy.

Using these research papers to help define your value proposition can put a parks, recreation, or tourism organization in an entirely different light. Are you providing fun, or are you central to the local economy? Is it leisure, or are you creating a healthier society, reducing health care costs, and increasing life spans? Is it recreation, or are you offering part of the solution to global warming or revitalizing a blighted community?

Green Sports

An Example of Positioning a Stadium as Important to the Environment

A large-scale example of what is possible for the future can be seen in hundreds of large sports stadiums across the county. College sports programs have long been an effort by high education institutions to position themselves in the minds of potential donors, students, and alumni. A successful season would result in many non-sports benefits for the institution. Today, an increasing number of colleges and universities are realizing that they can position themselves as environmental leaders in the minds of the fans, regardless of who wins the game. Hundreds of thousands of people attend collegiate games every year, and for a few hours, those people are within the environment of the stadium. If the college can demonstrate that you can have a great time and also have a lighter footprint on the natural world, that lesson is likely to affect those people in their lives away from the stadium.

One of many examples is The Ohio State University, which has high school students at "Zero Waste Stations" to help sports fans recycle most of their waste. They  switched to compostable trays and souvenir cups to be taken home instead of trashed. The result was a 98% reduction in the material that went into landfills from the stadium.

In 2013, more than 600 representatives from hundreds of colleges and universities attended a Green Sports Alliance Summit to share ideas on how to reduce waste, conserve energy and water, and demonstrate to the fans what is possible when some effort is put into sustainability.

By connecting collegiate sports with environmental sustainability, these stadiums have ramped up the role they are playing in society. They are no longer just a great place to have fun with your friends for a few hours. They are now cutting-edge examples of how to live in a more sustainable way. Already, the lessons learned in the stadium greening are helping to green other elements of campuses. In the longer run, demonstrating what is possible will affect thousands of individuals who will adopt more sustainable practices.

Many of the examples from this movement have been profiled in a national report called *Collegiate Game Changer: How Campus Sports is Going Green,* by the Natural Resources Defense Council: http://www.nrdc.org/greenbusiness/guides/sports/files/collegiate-game-changers-report.pdf

An entrepreneurial organization defines itself by its highest social and community values. The noble higher purpose feeds right back into a sense of mission, which feeds back into strategic planning and measurable results.

Here is another example of repositioning. It is a story that ran in the August 2013 issue of *Parks & Recreation Magazine* on the role park agencies can play in addressing global climate change from both the perspective of reducing our carbon footprint to being leaders in environmental education that goes beyond what parks and recreation agencies have traditionally done.

Nature is More than Birds and Bunnies

An Example of Positioning Parks as Important to Climate Change

The Role of Parks and Recreation in Global Climate Change

Parks have always had a role in nature education. They are where the public goes to experience and learn about the natural world. Many agencies have nature centers, guided hikes or paddling trips, nature-focused summer camps, and more. But most of those programs and facilities are focused on local flora and fauna (birds and bunnies). There has always been and will always be some demand for this. However, if parks and recreation are to remain relevant and important in our communities, we need to address the important issues of today. And in the environmental field, nothing is bigger than global climate change. From extreme weather events to rising sea levels to reduced crop yields, the effects of climate change are front-page news.

These planet-altering impacts are caused by greenhouse gases heating our atmosphere. It may all seem too global to address on a local level, but it is not, and park agencies can be local leaders in promoting sustainability and educating people about what they can do.

Reducing Your Footprint

In 2005, the Northern Virginia Regional Park Authority adopted energy conservation plans for each park. At the same time, it started tracking its car-

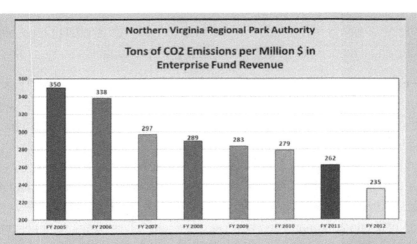

bon footprint. Using the accounting system, instead of just recording utility costs, it also recorded units of consumption for all fuels so it could calculate its carbon footprint. Every year, the facility that had the greatest reduction in energy consumption is recognized and awarded at an all-staff meeting.

Results. While carbon emissions in 2012 were virtually the same as in 2005, our park system has grown dramatically from 19 to 25 parks and from $10 to $16 million in enterprise revenues. With enterprise revenues as a good measure of activity, the Northern Virginia Regional Park Authority has been able to go from 350 tons of carbon per $1 million of enterprise revenue to just 235 tons. That indicates a great increase in efficiency!

How it was achieved. While many methods were used, the real answer to how it was achieved is the same answer to how anything is achieved: focus. In all aspects of life, you will go where you place your focus. In this case, focus has meant tracking results, creating plans, and making many small decisions that collectively move you in the direction you want to go. These small steps include the following:

- Having a policy that the "life cycle costs" of any energy consuming system are considered. This means that you might not buy the cheapest equipment if that equipment uses more energy in the long run.
- Addressing "low-hanging fruit" such as lighting and insulation to improve the energy consumption of existing buildings.
- Building new structures with green building elements that improve efficiency.

- Using a wide range of technologies such as geothermal heat pumps, electric and hybrid vehicles, solar panels, and programmable thermostats.

Educate the public. Reducing your carbon footprint is just a small part of the answer for park and recreation organizations. At least as important is our role in educating the public, so they can learn how to be more sustainable in their lives too.

In 2009, Potomac Overlook Regional Park in Arlington Virginia revamped its aging nature center. The new center has an energy theme throughout the exhibits, from the solar power that creates plant life throughout the whole chain of life up to humans and how we use energy. This center connects how we live to all life on our planet. It is a different approach from the dusty, taxidermied beavers of traditional nature centers. And it is an approach that connects nature to people in more relevant ways.

In 2013, the two all-LED holiday light shows the Northern Virginia Regional Park Authority operated used renewable energy credits purchased to offset their power consumption. This initiative came from a sponsorship deal with Dominion Power for the light show and is yet another opportunity to educate the public about carbon footprint and sustainability.

Park agencies have always had a key role in connecting people to the natural world. In a world where our natural environment is changing rapidly as a result of climate change, we need to change just as fast in how we connect with the public on these issues and offer leadership in how to be part of the solution.

Reenactment Provides Economic Boost for Region

An Example of Positioning Parks as Important to the Tourism Economy

On October 22, 2011, Ball's Bluff Battlefield in Leesburg hosted one of the signature events in Northern Virginia's commemoration of the Civil War. With approximately 1,000 uniformed reenactors representing both sides, and a jury of 2,000 spectators, the reenactment of the battle that took place 150 years earlier was a true spectacle, and its effect on those who attended was clearly visible. In addition to the great educational value of this event, it proved to be a big part of Virginia's second biggest industry: tourism.

With the help of Visit Loudoun, the authority on tourism in Loudoun County, NVRPA was able to determine that the economic effect of the Ball's Bluff Reenactment totaled roughly $100,000 in economic gain for the area.

"Heritage tourism is such an important driver for visitation, and Visit Loudoun is pleased to support events like the 150th Ball's Bluff Reenactment, not only for the immediate economic visitor spending impact, but also for the long-term benefit allowing visitors to experience a unique Civil War legacy that only Loudoun County offers," said Patrick Kaler, President and CEO of Visit Loudoun.

Ball's Bluff is just one of many historic parks spread across the Northern Virginia region that are owned and operated by NVRPA. Venues such as the Carlyle House in Alexandria, the W&OD Trail (which stretches from Shirlington all the way to Purcellville, Mt. Zion), and Aldie Mill and, of course, Temple Hall Farm and Ball's Bluff in Leesburg, blaze a brilliant trail through history with a strong focus on the Colonial and Federalist periods, as well as the Civil War. And they are but a fraction of NVRPA's regional history experience.

NVRPA, in cooperation with Fairfax County Government television, recently completed a documentary regarding this legacy. Entitled *Region Divided: Civil War in the Northern Virginia Regional Parks* and narrated by former CBS and NBC anchor Roger Mudd, the film looks at the relevance of NVRPA's many historic sites and the roles they played during the country's bloodiest conflict. Much of the footage used in the film's discussion of Ball's Bluff was taken during the October 22 reenactment.

Cate Magennis Wyatt, president of Journey Through Hallowed Ground Partnership, was thrilled that the reenactment was able to bolster interest in both local history and the local economy.

"Heritage Tourism is the largest employer within the Journey Through Hallowed Ground National Heritage Area," Wyatt said. "Specifically, 54,000 jobs rely on visitors coming our way. The remarkable efforts of the Northern Virginia Regional Park Authority, in partnership with the Loudoun 150th Commemoration Committee, have added over $100,000 to our local economy. This is a wonderful example of how we can increase the quality of life for all, as we commemorate our shared heritage."

The reenactment was part of a whole weekend of Civil War-related events, which began at Morven Park on Friday, October 21 and continued through the 22nd, finishing with a candle-lit battlefield illumination on Saturday evening. Soldiers camped at Morven Park, offering a living history demonstration on Friday, and then marched to Ball's Bluff for the reenactment. Spectators, who arrived from all over the region and farther away (at least one spectator was from Minnesota), parked at Morven and were bussed to Ball's Bluff. After returning to Morven at the end of the demonstration in the late hours of the afternoon, many descended upon Leesburg, taking advantage of the nearby town and enjoying the shopping, restaurants, and more.

"I sincerely believe that Loudoun's rich history and historical sites like the Balls Bluff Battlefield are great assets for the county," said Catoctin Supervisor-Elect Geary Higgins. "When you couple our history with the natural beauty, the wine country, and other rural economic resources, you have a very powerful tourist draw that will become a vital part of Loudoun's business tax base."

"We believe it's important to know that such a dynamic and important battle occurred so close to where many of us now live, work, and shop," said NVRPA board member and Leesburg resident, Joan Rokus. "We take parts of our history for granted, and this battle is the key reason why NVRPA acted to preserve this property."

18

Vision for the Future

Imagine Walking into the Agency Headquarters
20 Years from Today...

Before you get to the doors, you see a group of children emerging from a trail dirty and laughing after taking part in a naturalist-led adventure they are coming back from. The children's imaginations are fully engaged, as they joyfully interact. You can hear in their chatter that they have just learned some scientific principles and are excited that they were able to see them in the nature they have just been exploring.

You walk through the doors and instantly hear the talking and laughing of different sets of people engaged in conversation; many are smiling. People are walking rapidly down the hall with great purpose; you see a group that is engaged in developing plans for a new facility that is going to be the first of its kind in the region and will have some first-in-the-nation features. You see through glass doors a group of recreation programmers sharing the information  they recently presented at the NRPA Congress on best practices in the field. A level of optimistic excitement fills the room. You notice scrolled on the wall is the mission and elements of the strategic plan. Animated charts flash the progress toward each goal.

In a moment, a parade of local politicians comes in to get ready for the news conference where it will be announced that through the agency's efforts, tourism has increased 300% in the last decade, bringing jobs and prosperity to the region. Recognizing the great return on investment the taxpayers are getting, funding is being increased to the agency. As welcome as this news is, the proud agency employees already know that new parks, facilities, and programs have been added over the last few years funded out of 500% increase in enterprise revenue, and more are planned. At the news conference, the mayor mentions that a new poll shows that the parks and recreation agency is the most respected government agency by the public. The mayor also mentions how the growth of parks and their new and innovative uses has resulted in measurable positive impact in public health throughout the community. A doctor with the local hospital complex reinforces the message about the great savings in health costs and the close partnership between the park agency and the health care network.

If this vision is not your vision, that is okay. Write your own vision statement; do not limit yourself to what you think is practical today. Paint the picture that you would like to step into, and that will be your vision. Make your vision real and tangible; what does it look like, smell like, taste like, and feel like? Put yourself in the middle of the action, put it in the present tense, and state it in the positive. This kind of visioning is very powerful.

Okay, How Do We Get from Where We Are to Where We Want to Be?

This book started with the analogy of the Vikings and the farmers. Farmers were good managers who took the resources at hand (their fields) and did with them the best they could. This model works well in a static environment. If your field is always the same size, and you know you will have about the same amount of sunlight, water, and temperature, then you can do what you did last year and the year before that, and you will be okay.

This farmer model is where many parks and recreation agencies are today. They provide a set of services that has not changed substantially in many years, and they manage well the limited resources they are given. The national average is that most parks and recreation agencies generate 70% of their operating revenues from tax dollars and 30% from enterprise operations. So, if the tax base is not growing, the park agency is not likely to be in a growth mode. With efforts in many parts of the country to reduce taxes and shrink government, agencies that do not seem essential may be facing significant cuts.

A Bright Future of Growth

The bleak reality that some organizations find themselves in does not need to be. The secret to creating a brighter future is deceptively easy. While there are many steps and a lot of work involved in becoming a forward-looking, opportunity-creating (Viking) organization, the first and most critical step is focus. As with all elements in life, the first step is to envision where you want to go and then maintain a focus on this positive vision of the future. You can only see opportunities if you are looking for them! A great way to think about this is the simple task of riding a bike. If you look down the path or the road, that is where you will go, and if your focus is fixed on something to the side of you, you will veer off the path and crash. You go where your focus is.

Create an Indispensably Important Organization

Local parks, regional park districts, state and national parks, as well as local, regional, and national nonprofits and tourist destinations all create a sense of place. They have the ability to define what is special and important about where we live. Wow, what an amazing power! But whether an agency just operates a number of sites the way they always have done or realizes that they have a role in defining what is important about their community and their agency, makes all the difference. The agency that just mows the ballfields is largely insignificant, whereas the agency that keeps the community healthy and attracts tourism is indispensable. Make your agency indispensable by actively positioning it in the minds of the public.

Expand Your Funding

So, you have taken the first challenge and positioned your agency as truly important in the community. Congratulations! Now, how about a greatly expanded budget so you can do even more good in the world? From the good positioning of the organization, you might be on better footing to get more general operating (tax) funding. You might be able to win an expanded tax levy like Cleveland Metro Parks did. However, there is another great opportunity, that of self-funding.

School systems, fire, and police departments are almost entirely dependent on tax dollars, but not parks and recreation organizations. Some are, but few need to be. I believe that in most cases, public open space should be free to the tax payers who helped fund the public lands. However, while access to the lands should be free, park systems can and should create value-added services that engage the public in interesting and exciting ways. These value-added services should be priced and marketed to create the revenues that will help fund the other elements of the organization. While the national average is 30% of operating revenues generated from enterprise operations, the agencies that can generate 50%, 70%, or more of their operating revenues from enterprise are agencies that have created greater independence. They are much less dependent on taxpayer support and much less impacted by general local, state, and federal budgeting. And, if their enterprise revenue is diversified among a wide variety of operations, they have greater protection if one or more of the enterprise areas see a decline.

While not every agency will be able to self-fund the same amount, it is more about the journey than the destination. And it is not raising money for the sake of more funds, it is creating the ability to fund other beneficial projects that do not raise money in the community. So, the vision and goal should be to expand and diversify the funding sources. This is a liberating process of gaining greater control over the future health of the organization. And, to be successful at enterprise operations, an agency must be in touch with the customers and what they want. This drives an organization to be more nimble and responsive.

Build a Strong Team

While the talented individual is often celebrated, the greatest achievements in human history have all been the result of strong teams. The stronger the team, the more the organization will be able to achieve. There are many examples of organizations with tremendous resources at their disposal that failed, and other organizations with drive, spirit, and few other resources that changed the world for the better. So it is less about the size of your budget and staffing, and much more about your momentum that makes the difference.

Building that winning team has a lot to do with creating the vision and the plan that give purpose to the agency, and then hiring the best, cultivating and growing internal talent, and creating a work environment where people can see the progress and feel a part of something larger than themselves. When this happens, mountains can be moved.

Demonstrating Best Practices

Your agency is well positioned as being highly valuable, your enterprise revenues are growing with a sharp eye to what your customers want, and your team is pulling in the same direction with a strong sense of purpose! The next step that will keep the organization on top is to adopt and demonstrate the very best in organizational management. Look not at government, but at the best research sponsored by the top business schools in the nation. How can you market more like Apple, innovate more like Google, and provide customer service like Disney? Many of the greatest innovations come from adopting practices from across platforms or segments.

Best practices have a lot to do with how well internal functions operate. When the governance board is focused on the important policy and oversight issues, when budgets are a reflection of the strategic planning priorities of the organization and human resources are creating future leaders, then the overall strength and effectiveness of the organization grows.

Change the World

It may sound grandiose, but a high performance agency that is doing everything above everyone else is an amazing force for good in the world. The scope of that world may be local or regional, but such an organization can do amazing things, such as

- helping people to live healthy lives;
- revitalizing and defining communities;
- letting children learn interpersonal life skills through creative pro-gramming;
- educating the public about history, environment, and other important issues, making the world more sustainable;
- building character and confidence through completion;
- protecting our natural resources for future generations;
- creating places for wholesome fun and enduring memories;
- connecting children and nature; and
- creating new and exciting destinations.

People enter the field of parks and recreation, in government agencies or nonprofits, because they want to make a difference in their world and the lives of people. Those dreams are sometimes realized and sometime not, and much of the difference comes down to whether the organization is growing and becoming a high performance agency or is stuck in a static mode. So creating a high performance organization really does change the world for the better in so many ways. And in the process of changing the outside world for the better, every person involved in achieving that goal is changed for the better!

Leadership

"Be the change that you wish to see in the world."

—(often attributed to Mahatma Gandhi)

For the last 20 years, graduate business schools and top corporations have been focused a great deal on the difference between managers and leaders, very much like our analogy of Vikings and farmers. This movement that has spanned many books and classes was kicked off by former Harvard Business School Professor John P. Kotter in his 1992 article in the *Harvard Business Review,* "What Leaders Really Do." Before Kotter's work, MBA programs focused mostly on management, and since that time there has been much more of a recognition of the special role of leadership and how it differs from management.

Kotter saw three main differences between the two roles:

1. Planning and budgeting vs. setting direction
2. Organizing and staffing vs. aligning people
3. Controlling activities and solving problems vs. motivating and inspiring

Kotter saw most companies as overmanaged and underled. He wrote: "Consider a simple military analogy: A peacetime army can usually survive with good administration and management up and down the hierarchy, coupled with good leadership concentrated at the very top. A wartime army, however, needs competent leadership at all levels. No one yet has figured out how to manage people effectively into battle; they must be led." This analogy is very similar to the theme in this book that the farmer (manager) approach can work okay in a static environment, but in a changing environment the Viking (leader) organizations will be the high performance agencies that thrive.

Competent management is essential for any organization to function, but leadership is needed to grow and develop an agency.

Who Leads?

It is common for people to look at an organizational chart and assume the people at the top are the leaders. But in reality, sometimes this is true, and sometimes it is not. In the best-case scenarios, the people in leadership positions understand their roles and are well suited for them. In a high performance agency, both the people at the top of the organization and the people throughout the organization at all levels are involved in leadership.

This model can only work well if there is a clearly articulated, understood, and respected sense of vision and mission. When it is clear what the better future that is being created is, it frees people throughout the organization to provide leadership in their areas that complement and build on the larger organizational vision. Without this larger vision in place, different groups within the organization can easily be working at cross purposes. The "aligning" part of Kotter's leadership definition is that of making sure the different parts of the whole are all moving in the same direction.

Aligning is also about understanding individual differences and using the unique talents and aptitudes of people most effectively.

So, leadership is for everyone who recognizes that they, too, can contribute to achieving the vision. Few, if any, job descriptions say "achieve the vision." So if your focus is just on doing the job, you are not engaged in leadership, and while you might be doing many good and useful things, you are not helping to manifest the brighter future that is possible.

While organizations should be moving into flatter structures, information in a world of advanced web and mobile technology is being distributed on a very flat level. All of these structural changes create more leadership opportunities at every level in an organization. But such opportunities only result in leadership if people see them as opportunities and act on them.

Being a leader outside of a senior job has two great benefits. First, it moves the organization ahead to a brighter future, which changes the world in positive ways; but secondly, showing leadership is perhaps the single best thing that can be done to advance your career. Make the world a better place and advance your own career. That is a win-win! Let us explore how to show leadership.

Embrace the Vision

Since vision is the most important trait in leadership and organizational development, it is the most important thing to actively align your efforts to support. If you can look for ways that are within your power to move the vision and strategic plan forward, senior management will take notice and appreciate what you are doing. Help others around you to understand and live the mission and vision. Don't wait for someone to tell you what to do. Do all you can to understand the organizational direction and priorities, and look for ways you can initiate or support efforts to advance those goals.

If you are in an organization without strong leadership and a clear vision, then help to create that vision. Think about what the strengths of your organization are and what you could do that would achieve a higher goal. Explain this goal to others, ask your supervisor what he or she thinks, and try to share the idea with as many others as you can. Be open to changing or modifying this vision based on new information. If your priority is not widely accepted, look for another that has more buy-in. If you can help establish a goal for the future, and then help achieve it, you are a leader. If goals, mission, and vision already exist, do not try to push things in a different direction, but get behind the adopted vision and make it happen. None of this happens by just doing your job. Leadership like this only happens by stepping outside of the day-to-day tasks and thinking about and working on longer term objectives.

Strike the Right Balance

Being competitive can be good, but being a collaborative team builder is also good. The trick is that sometimes these two drives work counter to each other, and being too far on either side of this spectrum can limit your career and your leadership ability. Know when to use the competitive juices to motivate your group, and know when too much of it blocks the cooperation and collaboration that is needed to get the best results. Being overly collaborative and noncompetitive can be too passive. Ideally, you want to be a good team player who is aggressive enough to push yourself and others out of the comfort zone to achieve the vision.

Be an Agent of Change

The most powerful people in the world are those who have a foot in the current reality and a foot in the future and can help others see what is to come and help to create that new reality. Most people have both feet in the here and now. So, embracing the future and working to create a better one is an act of leadership.

Copernicus … Galileo … Darwin … Ford … the Wright Brothers. … None began with serious resources or backing. All created change through the power of their ideas.

Leaders have one foot in the present and one in the future, *and help others to bridge that gap.*

Senior Management

While there is no one formula, Kotter defines the several career traits that great leaders often have. He notes that many have had the opportunity to lead, take risks, and make important decisions in their 20s or 30s. And, of equal importance, many of these people have had a breadth of experience resulting from lateral moves and promotions. The early leadership shows them what can be done, and the breadth gives them a more holistic view of the organization and all the pieces of the puzzle. Extra training and education, and exposure to cross- functional teams can also help develop powerful leaders.

Most people who achieve senior management get there by first being a "subject matter expert." This means they were good at some skill set before they were promoted, perhaps even the best. Maybe they were the top facility manager, or a great planner, the top project manager, successful at land acquisition, or excellent at financial management. Whatever the skill set that led them to the senior position, they need to be able to let go of some of those areas they excelled in in order to take on the leadership role. This can be extremely difficult. When someone becomes an expert in something, they take pride in that and generally do not want to set that skill aside. But it is often necessary to do so, so they can focus on their new role.

Delegation and letting the little things go is absolutely essential to be an effective senior organization leader. The job is no longer to be the best at some technical skill, it is not to have an hand in every detail, it is to keep the focus on the big picture, inspire people to achieve the mission, and step in to help when some element of the operation needs to get unstuck from some problem. This role can be very difficult for many, because most people are "doers." There is always too much to do for the senior leader, but it is generally not the clearly defined tasks that dominate mid-level positions.

Some people do not understand this transition from worker bee "doer" to organizational rudder, cheerleader, and trouble shooter. When this shift is not made, organizations wind up with too many people trying to pull the ore, and no one paying attention to the rudder. If no one is keeping an eye on the mission and measuring the strategic plan, the organization will be adrift, and it might take years for people to realize opportunities have been lost and there has been no direction.

Think about the years Steve Jobs was the CEO of Apple Computers. He kept the whole organization clearly focused on its mission and vision, and as a result, they changed the world in remarkable ways. He did not spend most of his time writing computer code, finding a headquarters location with lower taxes, or writing the text for their advertising. A lesser CEO might have found comfort in immersing himself in comfortable tasks he was good at. And you can argue that any of those tasks, or countless other tasks that he could have engaged in would have been helpful to the company in some way. But all of those "in the weeds" kinds of jobs would have been a distraction from the primary job of a senior leader, that of keeping the organization on track. A high performance CEO keeps the focus on the big-picture progress of the organization, is always looking to where the next game-changing opportunity will come from, and making sure that the strategic decisions are being made that will move the organization forward.

Since many game-changing opportunities can come from new markets, new partnerships or new ideas, one of the primary tasks of a senior leader is to be engaged and networking outside of the organization. In many cases, senior leadership will be the face of the organization in community and professional network organizations. This gives that leader the opportunity to be a conduit of new ideas and connections from outside the organization that might help achieve some of the strategic goals. This falls into the opportunity-seeking role of the leader.

Executive training from the major business schools and the many excellent books on leadership can help a senior leader keep his focus where it needs to be. So much of everything in life comes down to intentionality. Where you put your focus is where you will go. If you focus on all the little problems and challenges, that is all you will see, and those little issues will

Leadership is a transformational role of

ushering in the future.

bring progress to a standstill. If you put your attention on what the various paths are to success, you will see more of those potential paths. Look for opportunities, and soon they will present themselves, maybe in ways that are unexpected. To be a leader is to rise above the details and look for the opportunities.

At any level in any organization, the role of leaders is to be a bridge between the here and now and the brighter future. It is a transformational job of ushering in the future. In the field of parks and recreation (and all the related fields) there is the potential to positively affect the whole community and all the people who live in that area. A strong and dynamic organization in this field can make a better world and transform lives in positive and important ways!

But this world of transforming potential can only be achieved by strong and dynamic organizations; organizations with a clear sense of mission and a plan to grow and achieve more. Since the beginning of time, humans have used organizations to achieve higher goals. The tribe provided a higher level of safety and security than the individual could achieve. Corporations, nonprofits, and governments allow for more resources to be focused on achieving defined goals. The stronger the organization, the greater their potential is to change the world.

You can change the world for the better by helping to build the strongest organizations with the best missions and visions for what can be.

The Science of Optimism
Why it is Essential for Leaders to Be Positive

Being positive is more than just an attitude, it is key to creating success. In a mega study of research on being positive, Lyubomirsky, King, and Diener (APA, 2005) found that people who were optimistic, energetic, and goal focused were happier and more successful in almost every element of life, including work. Their 2005 study, The Benefits of Frequent Positive Affect: Does Happiness Lead to Success?, found that positive optimistic people were more likely to achieve success at work, be reviewed well by their supervisors, and be focused on achieving goals (APA, 2005).

These findings correlate well with a different study by MIT study on nonverbal social signals conducted by Professor Alex "Sandy" Pentland (2008). Pentland measured various nonverbal communications traits such as voice inflection, eye contact, body language, and others and found that those who demonstrated energetic and positive interactions were much more successful at winning business deals and salary negotiations.

In extensive research conducted by the Gallup Organization (2009), it was found that when leaders make their employees feel enthusiastic about the future they are 69% more likely to be engaged in their jobs. This compares to just 1% engagement by employees when their leaders did not inspire hope. So, hope and optimism are more than just factors that effect individual performance. When we are around people who are positive, that feeling is contagious and will generate better morale and performance from everyone that is around the positive person. And when pessimism and lack of hope are present, that too is contagious.

Some portion of happiness and optimism is genetically predetermined, another portion is learned behavior. But there is some portion that is within our control. When people focus on positive things, remember when positive outcomes have happened in the past, it can build their optimism for the future. As long as we look at this as just an issue of an individual's mood it is not an important organizational issue. But when one looks at the social science that shows how such issues affect job performance of the group, it becomes a very big organizational issue.

Much about achieving great results has to do with putting great focus to those goals and that steps that will lead to success. This focus, problem solving, and attention is greatly aided by a belief that good results can and will happen.

References

Amabile, T., & Kramer, S. (2011). *The progress principle.* Cambridge, MA: Harvard Business Press.

American Psychological Association (APA). (2005). *Psychological Bulletin, 131*(6), 803–855.

Conchie, B. & Rath, T. (2009). Srength-based leadership. New York: The Gallup Press.

Golembiewski, R. T. (1985). *Humanizing public organizations.* Mt. Airy, MD: Lomond.

Haire, M., & Posey, R. (1961). Modern organization theory. *Administrative Science Quarterly, 5*(4), 609–611.

Kim, W. C., & Mauborgne, R. (2005). *Blue ocean strategy.* Cambridge MA: Harvard Business School Press.

National Infrastructure Financing Commission. (2012). *Falling behind: A crisis in transportation infrastructure investment.*

Pentland, A. (2008). *Honest signals.* Cambridge, MA: MIT Press.

Robertson, P. J., & Seneviratne, S. J. (1995). Outcomes of planned organizational change in the public sector: A meta-analytic comparison to the private sector. *Public Administration Review, 55,* 547–558.

About the Author

Paul Gilbert has been in leadership roles in government, nonprofit, and private sectors. He has served on the governance boards of six organizations and helped found two statewide associations.

Gilbert is the executive director of NOVA Parks (Northern Virginia Regional Park Authority) a multi-jurisdictional park system with a combined operating and capital budget of approximately $30 million and seasonally up to 1,000 employees. From 2005 to 2014, NOVA Parks grew its enterprise revenues by 75%, also conserving significant new areas of parkland, and adding new facilities.

Gilbert is an adjunct professor at George Mason University, where he teaches Administration of Park, Health and Tourism Organizations. He is the author of many published articles, as well as an award-winning book on leadership titled, *Lead Like a General*. Gilbert has been a keynote, and session speaker at numerous state and national conferences.

From 2009 to 2014, Gilbert served on the board of regents for the NRPA Revenue Development and Management School at Oglebay. From 2010 to present, Gilbert has served on the board of Visit Fairfax (Fairfax County Convention and Visitors Corporation) and was chairman of that tourism marketing organization in 2014.

In the past, Gilbert was the chief executive officer of a regional land conservation nonprofit, and also formerly was engaged in corporate acquisitions, government contracting, and marketing. Gilbert's diverse experience in public, private, and nonprofit sectors has contributed to his synthesized perspectives on what makes organizations in any sector succeed.

Contributors

Barbara Tulipane, Foreword
President, National Recreation and Park Association

John O'Meara, Land Acquisitions
Executive Director, Columbus and Franklin County Metropolitan Park District, Ohio

Tom Starnes, Earned Media
Communications Manager, Orange County Park District, California

Mary Beth Thaman, Financial Sustainability
Director, Kettering Department of Parks Recreation and Cultural Arts, Ohio

Brian Zimmerman, Winning the Levy
Chief Executive Officer, Cleveland Metro Park District, Ohio

Michael McCarty, Valhalla
Director, Fairfax City Park and Recreation Department, Virginia

Tom Lovell, A Crisis of Knowledge
Administrator, Lee's Summit Parks and Recreation Department, Missouri

Randall Ferris, Secrets of Farmers and Vikings
Senior Attractions Supervisor, Herschend Family Entertainment, Stone Mountain Park, Georgia

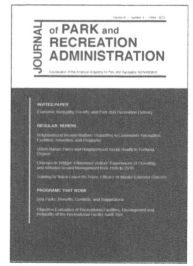